Contemporary Diagnosis and Management

The Patient With Schizophrenia

Henry A. Nasrallah, MD
Professor of Psychiatry, Neurology, and Medicine,
The University of Mississippi Medical Center,
and Chief of Mental Health Services,
Veterans Affairs Medical Center,
Jackson, MS

and

Donald J. Smeltzer, MA
Associate Professor of Psychiatry,
The Ohio State University College of Medicine,
Columbus, OH

Published by Handbooks in Health Care Co.,
Newtown, Pennsylvania, USA

Adelina Hills

Dedications

From Dr. Nasrallah: To Amelia, my wife and collaborator, who never ceases to amaze me with her many talents and to inspire me with her love and indomitable spirit.

From Professor Smeltzer: To my parents, from whom I have received so much, and A.M.D.G.

International Standard Book Number: 1-931981-02-7
Library of Congress Catalog Card Number: 2002102251

Table of Contents

This book has been prepared and is presented as a service to the medical community. The information provided reflects the published literature as well as the knowledge, experience, and personal opinions of the authors, Henry A. Nasrallah, MD, Professor of Psychiatry, Neurology, and Medicine, The University of Mississippi Medical Center, and Chief of Mental Health Services, Veterans Affairs Medical Center, Jackson, MS, and Donald J. Smeltzer, MA, Associate Professor of Psychiatry, The Ohio State University College of Medicine, Columbus, OH.

This book is not intended to replace or to be used as a substitute for the complete prescribing information prepared by each manufacturer for each drug. Because of possible variations in drug indications, in dosage information, in newly described toxicities, in drug/drug interactions, and in other items of importance, reference to such complete prescribing information is definitely recommended before any of the drugs discussed are used or prescribed.

Introduction

Schizophrenia is a complex disorder to define and study. Despite recent technical advances that have made it possible to visualize the structure and histochemical functioning of the living brain, our scientific data base remains incomplete. Gaps in knowledge are numerous, and old controversies persist.

In this book, we summarize current information on the manifestations, pathophysiology, and clinical management of schizophrenia. We also examine a few areas of controversy that involve especially important issues. While it is not possible to cover all topics comprehensively, we hope to provide information that is interesting and useful to a wide readership. We omit many details, as well as some topics of interest primarily to specialists.

Nearly all psychiatrists in the United States formulate diagnoses in accordance with the American Psychiatric Association's *Diagnostic and Statistical Manual of Mental Disorders*. Since 1980, this manual has defined and grouped mental illnesses according to descriptive clinical features alone, eschewing reliance on abstract theories and unproven etiologic assumptions. We follow the usual practice of referring to this important reference by the acronym DSM, and to its most recent (fourth) edition by DSM-IV. Similarly, ICD and ICD-10 refer to the *International Classification of Diseases*, published by the World Health Organization, and its most recent (10th) revision.

Readers who seek greater detail should consult the references listed in the Suggested Readings at the end of each section. However, *caveat lector*: schizophrenia research is advancing so rapidly that even the most thorough references become outdated on some topics soon after publication.

What Is Schizophrenia?

This question can be understood in many senses and answered at many levels. Here we provide a brief overview of schizophrenia as an introduction to the more detailed discussions that will follow.

Schizophrenia Is a Brain Disease.

It is not easy to give a precise definition of disease, but we use the term in the same sense that any physician would speak about diabetes, epilepsy, or breast cancer. Similarly, we follow the convention of using the singular form of the word, even though schizophrenia probably has etiologic and pathophysiologic variations.

Many people are familiar with nonmedical models of schizophrenia, but they often know little about the current disease model, or mistakenly believe that other models are still credible as alternative hypotheses. They may have learned, for example, that factors such as schizophrenogenic mothers, double-bind patterns of communication, marital schisms, defective ego boundaries, or oral fixation cause schizophrenia. They may respect the humanism implied by nonscientific explanations that schizophrenia is a 'problem in living,' a 'sane reaction to an insane world,' or a 'solution' discovered by troubled persons to escape from intolerable psychic pain. They may have heard political (antipsychiatric) assertions that schizophrenia is only a label used to control troubled or troubling persons, or that it is a myth whose function is to justify the profession and increase the income of psychiatrists, or even that it is merely an excuse for injury inflicted by means of psychiatric medications. Uncritical acceptance and dissemination of these ideas have caused harm to patients and their families. None is supported by scientific evidence.

In contrast, the disease model of schizophrenia is based on a burgeoning body of evidence that has had a leavening effect on all of neuroscience. Most important, it is the only approach that offers realistic hope to patients, their families, and society.

Schizophrenia Is a Psychotic Disorder.

Historically, the term *psychotic* has conveyed different meanings. Before 1980, it was often applied to any mental disorder causing severe impairment (a quantitative meaning). Alternatively, some clinicians considered the term *psychosis* interchangeable with schizophrenia, as if no other form of psychotic disorder existed.

Modern definitions emphasize an individual's loss of contact with external reality—that is, perceptions and interpretations of the world are irreconcilably different from those of other people. This definition is qualitative, not quantitative. In some psychotic disorders, patients may be able to conceal their impairment in reality testing, or their thoughts and behaviors may appear reasonable and plausible to others, or only limited areas of their mental lives are affected. In schizophrenia, however, there is usually a profound disorganization of mental functioning, so that external behavior seems bizarre to observers, and internal mental experiences are incomprehensible and frightening to the patient.

Such conditions are vividly described in ancient literature and have been observed throughout recorded history. They have sometimes been explained by religious or spiritual metaphors. More often, they have been fearfully referred to as 'madness.'

People with schizophrenia may experience psychotic breaks from reality intermittently or for continuous periods of long duration. Psychotic episodes are an essential feature of schizophrenia, but they are not unique to it, nor are they its only defining characteristics.

Schizophrenia Is Not 'Split Personality.'

Many people mistakenly understand schizophrenia as meaning 'split personality.' This was not the meaning intended by Eugen Bleuler, the Swiss psychiatrist who first proposed the term as a replacement for the older name *dementia praecox* (premature dementia).

Further, this misinterpretation confuses schizophrenia with the condition now called *dissociative identity disorder* (formerly known as multiple personality disorder). The latter involves the presence of two or more distinct identity or personality states that recurrently and alternately manifest themselves in a person's behavior. Each personality state can act rationally and generally remains in good contact with external reality. Compared with schizophrenia, this condition is far more rare and seldom as disabling. Even its existence is controversial.

An interpretation of schizophrenia closer to Bleuler's meaning would be *disconnected mind*. He proposed this term to highlight a lack of coherence in mental functioning that he believed to be the essential characteristic. This defect impairs the integration of various mental activities. Thinking, feeling, perceiving, behaving, and experiencing operate without the normal linkages that make mental life comprehensible and effective.

Bleuler went on to develop a specific theory to account for this fragmentation. His book, *Dementia Praecox, or the Group of Schizophrenias*, was extremely influential in psychiatry, particularly in the United States. His clinical observations and descriptions were remarkably astute. His theories are less important today, except for historical perspective. The term *schizophrenia,* however, has become the preferred designation for a group of devastating mental disorders.

Schizophrenia Comprises a Heterogeneous Group of Disorders.

Most clinicians and researchers agree with Bleuler that schizophrenia is heterogeneous. Like those with diabetes mellitus or mental retardation, patients with schizophrenia are similar in many important ways but show differences in cross-sectional clinical features, treatment response, and longitudinal clinical course. Sometimes the plural form of schizophrenia is used to emphasize that there likely are several (perhaps many) different etiologies and variations in pathophysiology. It is assumed that patients have distinctive characteristics that eventually will be useful for defining homogeneous groupings that predict differential treatment response. Until these distinctions are reliably identified, however, the disorders are grouped in a single category on the basis of the clinical features they share, and treatments remain relatively nonspecific.

The subtypes of schizophrenia listed in today's diagnostic manuals have historical significance and descriptive value, but it is doubtful that they correspond closely to differences in etiology or pathophysiology, and they have little importance for treatment selection. Delineation of the *internal* boundaries of the group of schizophrenias is still speculative and controversial.

Schizophrenia Has Uncertain Boundaries.

Only slightly less problematic than the internal boundaries of schizophrenia are the *external* boundaries. At one time, many psychiatrists diagnosed all 'nonorganic' psychosis as schizophrenia, because they considered delusions, hallucinations, thought process disorders, and other forms of impaired reality testing to be pathognomonic for it. Some included other forms of oddness, eccentricity, or nonconformity, even when these were not the result of grossly impaired contact with reality or a cause of severe functional impairment.

When psychiatric classification shifted from a theoretical system to an empirical one, these overinclusive approaches were replaced by criterion sets that delineated boundaries more precisely. Use of operational criteria improves diagnostic reliability, making the diagnosis of schizophrenia less dependent on the intuition or bias of the clinician. A disadvantage is that this approach implies that boundaries between disorders having similar clinical features are well validated. A high degree of certainty, however, is not justified by current knowledge.

DSM-IV proposes six criteria for the diagnosis of schizophrenia (see Chapter 3). The first three describe essential features that must be present (*inclusion criteria*), while the final three refer to other conditions with clinical similarities that must be ruled out (*exclusion criteria*) before diagnosing schizophrenia. Distinguishing schizophrenia from other conditions with clinical similarities is vitally important for the clinician, the patient, and the researcher. Exactly how to do so is still debated.

Some distinctions are widely accepted. Diagnoses of psychotic disorders attributable to the direct physiologic effects of general medical conditions, psychoactive substance use, or substance withdrawal take precedence over schizophrenia—that is, symptomatic (secondary) schizophrenia is not true schizophrenia. Similarly, diagnoses of mood disorders are generally given priority over schizophrenia.

Other distinctions are more tentative. The DSM-IV chapter on schizophrenia and other psychotic disorders lists schizophrenia, psychotic disorders due to general medical conditions, psychotic disorders due to psychoactive substance use or withdrawal, five other specific conditions, and a residual category. The corresponding section of ICD-10 lists more than a dozen other psychotic disorders. The differential diagnosis for schizophrenia is examined in Chapter 4.

Schizophrenia Impairs Brain Function.

Although most clinicians of the late 19th and early 20th centuries believed schizophrenia to be a disease of the brain, available technology was unable to identify specific lesions or even to demonstrate obvious abnormalities. As a result, nonbiologic theories were proposed by psychiatrists, psychologists, sociologists, anthropologists, and philosophers. Scientific efforts to validate these theories either were considered irrelevant or were as unsuccessful as biologic investigations had been, but many clinicians found the nonmedical theories intellectually and morally appealing. In the United States, some of these theories were respected by many and preferred by some until recently.

Today, it is neither credible nor humane to dispute that schizophrenias are diseases that alter the structure and impair the functioning of the brain. Many authors shorten this description to *brain disease*, but there are also viable hypotheses involving a primary locus of pathology outside the central nervous system (eg, in immunologic, gastrointestinal, or endocrine organs). Even these theories, however, recognize the brain as the final target of the disease process.

Schizophrenia Is Highly Disabling.

Schizophrenia causes significant disadvantages that make a person unable to function on a par with others. Although the term *disability* has negative connotations, the tendency today is to focus on positive expectations. Contrary to old stereotypes, many disabled persons function at nearly normal levels under the right circumstances, which usually involve environmental modifications and intensive habilitation or rehabilitation programs. This is also possible for some people with schizophrenia, although others remain extremely vulnerable and dependent in spite of vigorous, persistent, multifaceted intervention programs.

Schizophrenia entails a high risk for most of the misfortunes of modern life. Social consequences include isolation, ostracism, prejudiced mistreatment, unemployment, substandard housing, homelessness, poor education, and lack of essential human services. Legal adversities include being treated as a criminal rather than a sick person, as well as being an easy victim of crime, being victimized and exploited in other ways, and losing basic constitutional and human rights by prolonged nontherapeutic confinement. In Nazi Germany, patients with schizophrenia were subjected to eugenic policies that required involuntary sterilization and, later, total elimination. Health risks still include generalized increases in morbidity and mortality, the pathogenic effects of poor living conditions such as malnutrition and exposure to toxins and infectious agents, and reduced access to medical services. Psychiatric complications include lack of support systems, incorrect diagnosis, insufficient or ineffective treatment, substance abuse, other comorbidity, and suicide.

Suggested Readings

Technical, Scientific, and Medical References

American Psychiatric Association: *Diagnostic and Statistical Manual of Mental Disorders*: DSM-IV-TR, 4th ed. Washington DC, American Psychiatric Association, 2000.

Gottesman II: *Schizophrenia Genesis: the Origins of Madness*. New York, Freeman, 1991.

Hirsch SR, Weinberger DR, eds: *Schizophrenia*. Cambridge, Blackwell Science, 1995.

Johnstone EC, Humphreys MS, Lang FH, et al: *Schizophrenia: Concepts and Clinical Management*. Cambridge, Cambridge University Press, 1999.

Nasrallah HA, series ed: *Handbook of Schizophrenia*. Amsterdam, Elsevier, 1986, 1987, 1989, 1990, and 1992. Five volumes.

Books Suitable for Patients' Families

Green MF: *Schizophrenia Revealed: From Neurons to Social Interactions*. New York, WW Norton, 2001.

Jeffries JJ, Plummer E, Seeman MV, et al: *Living and Working with Schizophrenia*. Toronto, University of Toronto Press, 1990.

Torrey EF: *Surviving Schizophrenia: A Manual for Families, Consumers and Providers*, 3rd ed. New York, Harper Collins, 1995.

Tsuang MT, Faraone SV: *Schizophrenia: The Facts*, 2nd ed. Oxford, Oxford University Press, 1997.

Weiden PJ: *Breakthroughs in Antipsychotic Medication: A Guide for Consumers, Families, and Clinicians*. New York, WW Norton, 1999.

Chapter 1

History of Schizophrenia

L ike diabetes or epilepsy, schizophrenia has been described, defined, diagnosed, and explained in many different ways. Opinions about its essential clinical features have varied greatly. Even today, definitions range from narrow to broad and are based on various combinations of empirical data and abstract theories. Diagnostic practices may emphasize longitudinal patterns, cross-sectional features, or some combination.

The fourth edition of the *Diagnostic and Statistical Manual of Mental Disorders* (DSM-IV—see Introduction) recommends diagnosing schizophrenia by criteria that are narrow, empirical, and atheoretical (ie, not based on unproved theoretical assumptions). Both cross-sectional and longitudinal features are included. *The International Classification of Diseases*, 10th revision (ICD-10—see Introduction) provides diagnostic criteria for research that are similar to the DSM-IV criteria but are somewhat broader. Although these approaches are scientifically grounded and widely accepted, Andreasen cautions against the 'ahistorical fallacy' of assuming that recent practice is always more valid than previous practices. Some old controversies about schizophrenia remain unresolved, including disagreements about its definition and diagnosis.

The Origin of Schizophrenia

One controversy concerns whether schizophrenia is ancient or recent in origin. Fictional and nonfictional literary works dating to the second millennium BC contain descriptions of psychotic illness, but they lack sufficient information for diagnosis according to modern standards. Many scholars believe that some of the patients described were suffering from schizophrenia and that the condition has existed in recognizable (though not necessarily static) form for several millennia. Timothy Crow, for example, attributes the origin of schizophrenia to the 'speciation event' that established humanity as a separate species. E. Fuller Torrey, on the other hand, argues that schizophrenia either did not exist or was extremely rare until 200 years ago and links its appearance to the industrial revolution. Each of these hypotheses is cogently argued and is supported by some evidence but must still be considered highly speculative.

The predominant opinion today is that schizophrenia is an old disease of unknown origin. It is also believed that important characteristics of schizophrenia have gradually changed over time.

Pinel, Haslam, and Morel

The oldest descriptions of indisputable schizophrenia were published during the first decade of the 19th century by Philippe Pinel in France and John Haslam in England.

Describing his observations in the two largest asylums in Paris, Pinel (1745-1826) proposed five categories of mental disorders. Although his groupings do not correspond closely to our own, he described many patients who certainly would meet modern criteria for schizophrenia. Most of these were included in a category he called *démence*, "the abolition of the thinking faculty."

In England, John Haslam (1764-1844) wrote about "a form of insanity which occurs in young persons." Haslam was superintendent of Bethlem Royal Hospital in London; our word *bedlam*, a synonym for madhouse, was derived from this name. Without describing particular patients, Haslam wrote a summary based on observations of many cases. Sufficient details were included to convince modern readers that he was describing schizophrenia, although he did not suggest any specific name for this condition. Some English psychiatrists today refer to schizophrenia as *Pinel-Haslam disease.*

Benedict Augustin Morel (1809-1873), an Austrian psychiatrist, reported cases of young persons who had fallen prematurely into dementia, a condition he referred to as *démence juvénile.* In 1860 he published a detailed report of an adolescent boy who had once been bright, active, and intelligent. The boy began behaving bizarrely, became progressively more withdrawn, and then deteriorated intellectually until, "a sudden paralysis of the faculties, a *démence précoce*, indicated that this patient had reached the end of the part of his intellectual life that he could control."

Kahlbaum and Hecker

In Germany, Karl Kahlbaum (1828-1899) endorsed the longitudinal study of clinical course and outcome in patients as a strategy for identifying characteristic features of mental diseases. He is best remembered for describing *catatonia* (tension insanity), a condition characterized by periods of rigid postures and mutism. Similarly, his student Ewald Hecker (1843-1909) described a psychosis in which the patient displays inappropriate, silly mannerisms; extremely regressed behavior; and nonsensical thinking. He named the condition *hebephrenia* (child-like insanity).

Emil Kraepelin: Longitudinal Diagnosis by Course and Outcome

The descriptive approach to classification of psychoses was significantly advanced by Emil Kraepelin (1856-1926), who wrote nine editions of a textbook considered a classic of scientific psychiatry. In 1918, he founded a psychiatric research institute in Munich that was the first of its kind in the world. His ideas about classification of mental disorders are still influential today.

Kraepelin agreed with Kahlbaum that, until definitive laboratory tests or neuropathologic findings have been discovered, the longitudinal study of a disease is an effective strategy for differentiating its 'essence' (essential characteristics that uniquely identify it) from its 'accidents' (nonspecific characteristics that are less diagnostically useful). He collected detailed information about the course of patients' conditions over time, expecting that such data would be useful for identifying distinct disease entities that might eventually be shown to have characteristic anatomic pathologies.

In 1898, he suggested that *démence précoce*, catatonia, hebephrenia, and a condition he had previously called *dementia paranoides* might all be subtypes of a condition resulting from a single morbid process. His rationale (later disputed by Bleuler) was that all these conditions begin early in life and progressively deteriorate to a common end stage. He proposed *dementia praecox* (premature dementia), the Latin form of Morel's term, as a suitable name. In the sixth edition of his textbook (published in 1899), he differentiated it from *manic-depressive insanity*, which shows a characteristic course of relapses and remissions, typically with full recovery of functioning between episodes.

Although his definition of dementia praecox was based on a dismal outcome, Kraepelin suggested cross-sectional diagnostic guidelines. He described bizarre thought disturbances, delusions, auditory or other hallucinations, catatonia, abnormalities of volition, and "a pervasive reduction in cognitive and affective capacity" as characteristics useful for its diagnosis. He also called attention to "peculiar states of mental weakness" that he believed were an essential feature, the unifying link that justified grouping these categories together. By this he meant that patients with dementia praecox, unlike those with senile or arteriosclerotic dementia, seemed not to actually lose their mental abilities, but rather to become unable to use them appropriately.

Kraepelin was fascinated by the psychologic features of dementia praecox, but he believed these were not useful for identifying its true cause. He therefore refrained from speculating about cause-and-effect relationships among symptoms, and he stated that it was the presence of certain symptoms, not their content or meaning, that was clinically significant. He restricted his theorizing to a belief that a disease process affecting cortical neurons was present. He conceded that a small proportion of patients (initially he estimated 2.5%) were capable of full recovery and that a similar small proportion might experience onset in middle or late age rather than in adolescence or early adulthood.

Eugen Bleuler: Cross-Sectional Diagnosis by the Four A's

Kraepelin's definition of dementia praecox was challenged, expanded, and then fundamentally changed by Eugen Bleuler (1857-1939), who had been an associate of Sigmund Freud.

In *Dementia Praecox, or the Group of Schizophrenias*, published in 1911, Bleuler argued that Kraepelin's definition was too narrow, that the words *dementia* and *praecox* were inaccurate, and that the condition was not a single disease but a heterogeneous grouping. According to Bleuler, onset in adolescence and dementia-like deterioration were seen only in the most severe cases. He agreed that severe impairment might be caused by brain lesions, but he stated that most cases were mild. In the latter it was possible that no brain lesion existed, and that the symptoms were caused by merely quantitative deviations from normal brain function. Kraepelin's recommendations for diagnosis would not be applicable in these cases.

The term *schizophrenia* referred to the loss of mental connectedness that Bleuler believed to be its essential characteristic. He attributed this fragmentation to a mental mechanism he called *associative splitting*, and he described fundamental symptoms of schizophrenia that demonstrated its presence. He argued that these symptoms were relatively specific for schizophrenia, were present in all patients who have schizophrenia, and were evident (though perhaps in mild form) at all stages of the disorder. Other features, including those emphasized by Kraepelin, were only accessory symptoms in the sense that they were caused by the fundamental symptoms, were not specific for schizophrenia, and were present only in some cases.

Four of Bleuler's fundamental symptoms have been called the four A's of schizophrenia (Table 1-1). He defined the combination of all four as pathognomic for schizophrenia. Later, he considered 'thought disorder' alone to be pathognomonic.

Bleuler accepted Kraepelin's subtypes of catatonic, hebephrenic, and paranoid schizophrenia. Because he believed that delusions and hallucinations were not essential for the diagnosis, he described two additional subtypes that lacked those features.

In *simple schizophrenia*, personality and functioning deteriorate substantially, but accessory symptoms such as hallucinations and delusions never develop. Bleuler stated that persons with simple schizophrenia often survived as "day laborers, peddlers, even as servants."

The largest of Bleuler's subtypes was *latent schizophrenia*, which consisted of all the 'milder' cases. He described this group as "irritable, odd, moody, withdrawn, or exaggeratedly punctual people." Most of these persons would today meet diagnostic criteria for having personality disorders (especially schizoid or schizotypal), anxiety disorders, or no psychiatric diagnosis at all.

Bleuler's concept of schizophrenia was more dimensional than categorical. All four of the fundamental symptoms occur on a continuum with normality, without clear cutoffs. It is possible to find evidence of their presence in every person. For this reason the diagnosis was greatly

Table 1-1: Bleuler's Fundamental Symptoms of Schizophrenia (The Four A's)

• *Association defects:* fragmentation and disconnection in the formation and expression of thoughts. Bleuler often referred to this symptom by the general term *thought disorder*.

• *Autism:* use of primitive mental processes that are archaic, illogical, and influenced by symbolic wishes and fears, similar to dreaming. When severe, it can cause the person to withdraw interest from the external world, resulting in preoccupation with private mental experiences, even to the exclusion of all else.

• *Ambivalence:* simultaneous experience of two impulses, wishes, thoughts, or emotions that are diametrically opposed. The result ranges from mild interior discomfort to erratic and unpredictable behavior to full volitional paralysis.

• *Disturbance of affect:* emotions displayed are inappropriate to the situation or inconsistent with thoughts expressed. Common abnormalities include affect that is constricted in range, blunted or flattened in amplitude, or inappropriate in character to the situation.

dependent on the judgment (or the opinion or bias) of the clinician.

Freud's ideas and approaches were received more enthusiastically in the United States than in Europe, and Bleuler's concept of schizophrenia also found wide acceptance here. Before the publication of DSM-III in 1980, many clinicians diagnosed schizophrenia by the four A's. As a result, the diagnosis was recorded more frequently in this country than in any other.

In Germany, Bleuler's term *schizophrenia* gained general acceptance, and his additional subtypes were accepted by Kraepelin and listed in his book. Bleuler's psychologic approach to diagnosis, however, remained less influential than Kraepelin's purely descriptive method.

Kurt Schneider: First-Rank Signs

A third approach that became popular in the middle of the 20th century was based on phenomenology, an existential theory of psychopathology that focused on understanding and describing a person's interior experience. In 1937, Kurt Schneider (1887-1967) proposed a simple method for applying phenomenologic concepts to the diagnosis of schizophrenia. He described 11 'first-rank' signs that indicated "a lowering of the barrier between the self and the surrounding world." He claimed these are highly specific for schizophrenia and are seen frequently enough to have practical diagnostic application. They are described in Table 1-2.

Schneider explained that "the value of these symptoms is…only related to diagnosis; they have no particular contribution to make to the theory of schizophrenia, as Bleuler's basic and accessory symptoms have. When any one of these modes of experience is undeniably present and no basic somatic illness can be found, we may make the decisive clinical diagnosis of schizophrenia. Any one of these signs, however, may sometimes occur in psychotic states that arise from a known physical illness: alcoholic psychoses, for example."

He acknowledged that other first-rank signs might also exist, that first-rank signs are not present in all cases of schizophrenia, and that diagnosis must sometimes be based only on second-rank signs (clinical features that are less specific). The priority of Schneider's first-rank signs in diagnosing schizophrenia became widely accepted. Even today, DSM-IV and ICD-10 attribute special significance to them. Studies find that 50% of patients with schizophrenia show one or more of these signs and that they are much less frequent in other psychotic conditions. They are not, however, pathognomonic of schizophrenia.

Schizophrenia in the United States Before DSM-III

In the United States, there were wide variations in diagnostic practices. Schizophrenia was not the only controversial diagnosis, but it was among the more troublesome. The approaches of Kraepelin, Bleuler, and Schneider were all in use. Prominent American psychiatrists, notably Adolf Meyer and Harry Stack Sullivan, proposed further refinements. Several distinct schools of psychoanalysis were flourishing, and each had its own theory of schizophrenia. Some clinicians used idiosyncratic approaches.

Many American psychiatrists favored the diagnosis of schizophrenia for virtually all 'nonorganic' illnesses that included delusions, hallucinations, or 'thought disorder.' The diagnosis was used for brief and prolonged illnesses. It was extended also to conditions involving exclusively nonpsychotic features—especially impaired functioning, flattened affect, poor interpersonal relationships, and unusual behavior. Some applied it to virtually any mental disorder that did not respond to psychoanalytic treatment or included 'loss of ego boundaries.'

It became apparent that the diagnosis of schizophrenia was more frequent in the United States than anywhere else in the world. Studies during the 1960s sought to determine whether this discrepancy resulted from true differences in prevalence or—as many observers suspected—from arbitrary differences in diagnostic practices. The findings strongly favored the latter interpretation.

This conclusion was further supported by the World Health Organization's (WHO) International Pilot Study of Schizophrenia. In seven of nine countries participating, the WHO found close agreement on the clinical features that led to a diagnosis of schizophrenia. The two outliers were the United States and the USSR. Both had approaches far broader than the other seven (and also different from each other).

These findings increased the urgency felt by many who were seeking to restore the scientific credibility of psychiatry. New approaches to diagnosis were proposed, utilizing

Table 1-2: Schneider's First-Rank Symptoms of Schizophrenia

Special auditory hallucinations
- *Audible thoughts (thought echo):* voices speak the person's thoughts aloud or comment on them.

- *Voices arguing:* Two or more voices argue or discuss, usually with the person as the subject and referred to in the third person.

- *Voice commenting:* A voice describes or comments on the person's activities as they occur.

Special delusions
Autochthonous (apophanous) experiences
- *Delusional perception:* The person attributes a specific, delusional, idiosyncratic meaning to a normal perception. The content is usually elaborate and self-referential and is experienced as a sudden revelation (apophany) or insight. It is not an inference based on previous experience.

Passivity experiences
- *Somatic passivity (made sensations, alien penetration):* The person experiences bodily sensations (sometimes hallucinatory) as imposed by outside forces, perhaps by some extraordinary means such as irradiation or psycho-kinesis.

structured interviews and systematic data-gathering. Attention was focused on symptoms considered easily recognizable and highly discriminating, such as Schneider's first-rank symptoms. Formal operational criteria (decision rules) were developed for translating clinical data into diagnostic assignments. Most criterion sets were organized hierarchically—that is, they included exclusion criteria clarifying which diagnoses should have priority.

Passivity experiences (continued)
- *Passivity of affect (made feelings):* Some outside agency imposes on the person emotions or affects that are not the person's own.
- *Passivity of impulse (made impulses or drives):* Some outside agency imposes on the person drives, impulses, or wishes that are not the person's own.
- *Passivity of volition (made volitional acts):* The person's motor activity is controlled by some outside agency.

Alienation of thought
- *Thought withdrawal:* Some outside agency removes the person's thoughts.
- *Thought insertion (made thoughts):* Some outside agency inserts thoughts into the person's mind.
- *Thought broadcasting (thought diffusion):* The person's thoughts passively diffuse into the environment and can be heard or experienced by others.

Psychiatry in the United States changed profoundly when the DSM-III was published in 1980. This edition differed radically from its predecessors by defining and grouping mental illnesses according to descriptive clinical features alone, rather than basing classification and diagnosis on theories of mental functioning and unproven etiologic assumptions. Widespread acceptance of disease definitions and diagnostic criteria based on observed clinical features brought unity and coherence to clinical practice, greatly improved the reliability of psychiatric diagnosis, and shifted debate from abstract theories to concrete data.

Revisions of the DSM after 1980 made further simplifications in the diagnosis of schizophrenia. Chapter 3 examines the criteria from DSM-IV.

Recommended Readings

Andreasen NC: Changing concepts of schizophrenia and the ahistorical fallacy. *Am J Psychiatry* 1994;151:1405-1407.

Bleuler E: *Dementia Praecox or the Group of Schizophrenias.* Zinkin J, trans. New York, International Universities Press, 1950.

Crow TJ: Is schizophrenia the price that *Homo sapiens* pays for language? *Schizophr Res* 1997;28:127-141.

Howells JG, ed: *The Concept of Schizophrenia: Historical Perspectives.* Washington DC, American Psychiatric Press, 1991.

Jeste DV, del Carmen R, Lohr JB, et al: Did schizophrenia exist before the eighteenth century? *Compr Psychiatry* 1985;26:493-503.

Schneider K: *Klinische Psychopathologie [Clinical Psychopathology],* 5th ed. Hamilton MW, trans. New York, Grune & Stratton, 1959.

Torrey EF: *Schizophrenia and Civilization.* New York, Jason Aronson, 1980.

Warner R, de Girolamo G: *Epidemiology of Mental Disorders and Psychosocial Problems: Schizophrenia.* Geneva, World Health Organization, 1995.

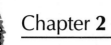

Chapter 2

Epidemiology and Risk Factors for Schizophrenia

Difficulties in Studying the Epidemiology of Schizophrenia

Problems of detection, definition, and diagnosis complicate epidemiologic studies of schizophrenia. Because there is no pathognomonic clinical finding, laboratory abnormality, or pathologic marker, the cooperation and self-report of affected people are necessary to recognize its presence. As examined in Chapter 1, different definitions of schizophrenia have been proposed, and each leads to a different method for arriving at diagnosis. Studies using different standards may produce substantially different results for this reason alone. For example, reports in the mid-20th century that schizophrenia was diagnosed more frequently in the United States than in other countries seem to be best explained in this manner.

Variations in study methodology can also lead to differences in frequency estimates. Some studies search for schizophrenia in medical records only, others evaluate patients from present hospital or clinic populations, others rely on community searches for disabled patients, and still others attempt direct sampling of community members. The latter may produce underestimates if the sampling method neglects persons without a fixed residence or those living in prisons, hospitals, nursing homes,

> ### Table 2-1: Possible Epiphenomena of Schizophrenia
>
> - Social isolation, ostracism, and stigma
> - Homelessness
> - Poverty and unemployment
> - Alienation from family or living in a disturbed or unstable family structure
> - Loss of freedom by prolonged confinement, possibly in poor institutional environments
> - Abuse, exploitation, victimization, and violence
> - Poor access to social services and medical care
> - Dietary deficiencies and abnormalities
> - Exposure to infections and toxins
> - Exposure to antipsychotic medications

homeless shelters, or geographically isolated regions. Diagnostic interviews may involve varying degrees of structure and may be conducted by skilled clinicians or by less-trained technicians.

Another problem involves epiphenomena that may be consequences rather than causes of schizophrenia and its true risk factors. For example, living in poverty may be a cause of schizophrenia or a consequence of schizophrenia, so the frequent finding that persons with schizophrenia are concentrated in the slums of large urban areas may be interpreted in different ways. Table 2-1 lists some conditions believed to be epiphenomena of schizophrenia.

Finally, because the age period of risk for schizophrenia extends over at least 40 years, one must be cautious when comparing statistics from populations that may have significantly different age distributions.

Incidence, Prevalence, and Morbid Risk for Schizophrenia

The *incidence* of a disorder refers to the rate of onset of new cases, usually measured as the number of new cases per 100,000 population members per year. As summarized in an extensive review by Warner and de Girolamo, most studies of schizophrenia diagnosed by 'standard' methods (similar to ICD-10 or DSM-IV) in community samples have reported age-corrected annual incidence rates between 10 and 40 new cases per 100,000 population.

The *prevalence* of a disorder is the proportion of population members affected at a given time (point prevalence) or during a specified time (period prevalence). Prevalence rates of a disease are a function not only of incidence rates, but also of chronicity, migration, and mortality. Warner and de Girolamo found a wide range of point prevalence rates of schizophrenia, ranging from 100 to 1,700, with a mean of 580, per 100,000 population members.

To evaluate the importance of possible risk factors for schizophrenia, the figure most often used for comparison is the *morbid risk*, defined as the proportion of a population meeting criteria for schizophrenia at any time during life provided they live through the entire age range of risk. Estimates of the morbid risk of schizophrenia range from 0.5% to 1.5%, and most authors use 1.0% as a suitable average. Table 2-2 summarizes the figures quoted above.

Geographic Variations in Rates of Schizophrenia

Prevalence rates of schizophrenia are significantly lower in undeveloped and underdeveloped regions than in highly industrialized areas. Lower incidence rates are also sometimes reported, but this is less consistent and does not adequately explain the lower prevalence rates. The more likely explanation, also supported by epidemiologic studies, is that the disease is milder and briefer in less industrialized regions. The pattern of a single episode of psychosis, with relatively complete recovery, good

Table 2-2: Basic Epidemiologic Estimates for Schizophrenia (Worldwide)

- Age-corrected annual incidence: 10 to 40 new cases per 100,000 population
- Age-corrected point prevalence: 100 to 1,700 cases per 100,000 population
- Lifetime morbid risk: 0.5% to 1.5% (average 1.0%)

subsequent functioning, and no further episodes, is seen significantly more often in these areas, so lower chronicity probably contributes to the reduced prevalence. Protective factors such as more supportive community environments, more cohesive extended families, and greater tolerance for nonproductive individuals may explain the lesser severity of the disease and enable some persons to recover without being classified as cases. Finally, severe schizophrenia leads to increased mortality, perhaps especially in third-world countries.

The prevalence of schizophrenia seems exceptionally high in a few populations, notably in Croatia, in northern Finland and Sweden, in native populations of northern Canada, and in the aboriginal peoples of Australia. High incidence rates have been found in parts of Ireland. Unusually low prevalence of schizophrenia has been found on Pacific islands and in the Amish and Hutterite communities in the United States.

A few authors argue that these differences are related to important causal factors and should be studied more closely. Torrey, for example, called attention to the possibility of a north-south gradient in distribution, similar to multiple sclerosis. Most epidemiologists, however, attribute the differences to nonetiologic factors such as those examined previously and conclude that worldwide distribution of schizophrenia is remarkably uniform.

Associations with Sociodemographic Variables
Age and Sex

Almost all available data suggest that men and women have the same morbid risk (around 1%) for schizophrenia. The distribution of age of onset (usually taken as age at time of first hospitalization), however, shows significantly different patterns for the two sexes.

For men, the average age of onset is between 20 and 25 years. The distribution peaks sharply between 20 and 25 years, shows a less prominent second peak between 30 and 35 years, and then falls off smoothly.

For women, most studies report an average age of onset about 5 years older than for men. The distribution shows peaks in the same age ranges as for men, but the peaks for women are approximately equal in height and significantly smaller than the first peak for men. After age 45, the ratio of new cases in women to new cases in men is at least 2:1.

Not only do women show onset of schizophrenia at a later average age than men, they also seem likely to have milder forms of the disease. Compared with averages for men, women with schizophrenia tend to have better premorbid functioning, fewer abnormalities on brain scans, shorter hospital stays, more complete recovery following episodes of psychosis, and better therapeutic response to antipsychotic medication. These findings have been confirmed by many studies and seem independent of the specific diagnostic approach used. They appear to be true across all cultures and to be specific for schizophrenia, not for mental disorders in general. They have never been adequately explained, but current theories suggest modulatory effects by estrogen on D_2 dopamine receptors. Another hypothesis is that earlier central nervous system maturation in females provides some protection against later development of schizophrenia.

Location of Residence and Social Class

The prevalence of schizophrenia is much greater in densely populated, large, urban areas of industrialized countries than in smaller cities, suburban areas, rural regions, and nonindustrialized countries. Within large urban areas, persons with schizophrenia are concentrated in areas of poorest housing conditions and have greatly increased possibility of being homeless. This pattern is not completely explained by differences in likelihood of seeking treatment or by selective relocation or migration. Possibly some factors in the environment of industrialized urban areas (perhaps the intensity of competition for resources) contribute to the onset or chronicity of schizophrenia.

In Western countries, schizophrenia is more prevalent among persons in the lowest socioeconomic groups. Although it is possible that poverty has some role in causation of schizophrenia, a causal relationship is more often hypothesized in the opposite direction. The *social drift hypothesis* proposes that schizophrenia renders a person unable to compete effectively for resources, resulting in downward social mobility (ie, a decline in socioeconomic status), or blocking the possibility of upward mobility. This hypothesis is supported by the distribution of socioeconomic status among fathers of probands with schizophrenia. The social class of the fathers is much closer than that of the probands to the general population.

In a few regions of India and other non-Western countries, schizophrenia is found more frequently in upper socioeconomic groups. Explanations for this finding are more speculative.

Marital Status

Schizophrenia is more prevalent among persons who have never married than among married persons of the same age. Divorce and separation are associated with a similar but smaller increase in prevalence. Two hypothesized explanations may each be partially correct. One is that having schizophrenia or vulnerability to schizophrenia selects against marriage. Unmarried people who have schizophrenia tend to have poorer premorbid functioning, earlier age of onset of psychosis, and more severe illness than those who are married; these associations are stronger in men than women. Possibly marriage (perhaps any close interpersonal relationship) may shield some vulnerable persons from the onset of schizophrenia.

Immigration Status, Ethnicity, and Race

Some studies, especially in western Europe, find a greater prevalence of schizophrenia in populations that have recently migrated than in either the country of origin or the country of new residence. Possible explanations include selective migration by persons of high vulnerability; causal stresses that precede, accompany, or follow the migration; and an increase in risk for misdiagnosis because of cultural and language differences. Findings of this sort may also be erroneous if investigators underestimate the size of the immigrant group being studied, leading to an overestimate of prevalence because the denominator (population size) is too small.

After the first generation of immigrants, the prevalence of schizophrenia tends to normalize. An interesting exception was found in studies of Afro-Caribbean immigrants to Great Britain, who showed a markedly increased rate of hospitalization for schizophrenia. Their offspring, although born and reared in Britain, showed an even greater increase of schizophrenia.

In the United States, black Americans were once believed to show excess prevalence of schizophrenia. More recent studies disprove this conclusion and attribute the older findings to racially biased diagnostic practices. Today it is believed that nonimmigrant minority groups have no greater risk for schizophrenia than the general population.

Risk Factors for Schizophrenia: Family and Genetic Studies

More than 80% of persons with schizophrenia have no affected relatives within the first degree of kinship (parents, children, or siblings), and more than 60% have family histories that are completely negative. Nevertheless, it has been established beyond a doubt that schizophrenia is a familial disease, and only a few skeptics remain unconvinced that this is determined more by genetic transmission than by environmental factors.

In a meticulous review of family studies of schizophrenia, Gottesman pooled data from 40 of the best studies done in Germany, Switzerland, the Scandinavian countries, and the United Kingdom between 1920 and 1987. Similar conservative diagnostic standards had been used, and data were relatively complete because of stable populations and availability of extensive case registers from public health services. The results of his calculations are displayed in Figure 2-1.

Gottesman concluded that the differences in risk across the various categories of relatives closely parallel the proportion of genes shared with a sick relative. He argued that parents have the lowest relative risk among first-degree relatives because severe schizophrenia greatly reduces reproduction; thus, affected parents would tend to have mild cases of the disease. Also, the much greater risk among offspring of dual matings (in which both parents have schizophrenia), compared with children who have only one parent with schizophrenia, is consistent with the former having received a 'double dose' of vulnerability.

The nearly threefold discrepancy between concordance rates for monozygotic versus dizygotic twins strongly suggests that sharing genes is more important than other similarities of twinship, including sharing an intrauterine environment. All of the studies used in calculating these concordances used modern procedures for determination of zygosity and long periods of follow-up to ensure that all affected co-twins were detected. Gottesman and Shields also analyzed the relationship between severity of illness and concordance for schizophrenia in monozygotic twins. Using several different indicators of severity, they concluded that concordance was much greater when the index twin showed a severe form of the illness than when the illness was mild.

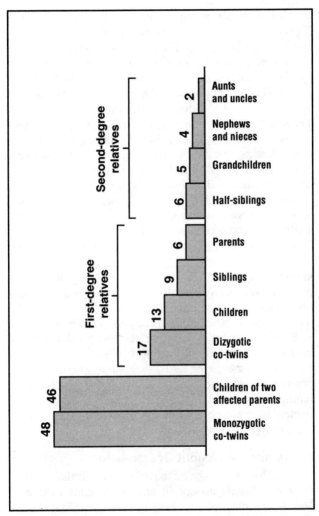

Figure 2-1: Relative risks for schizophrenia among family members of people with schizophrenia. (Modified from Gottesman II: *Schizophrenia Genesis: The Origins of Madness.* New York, WH Freeman and Company, 1991.)

Because the concordance rate for monozygotic twin pairs is only about 50%, nongenetic factors must also be important in the pathogenesis of schizophrenia. Various hypotheses might explain this finding, but the one best supported by available data involves a 'diathesis-stress' model of causation. This model proposes that genetic factors establish only the level of risk for development of schizophrenia. The risk determines a threshold of vulnerability that ranges across a continuum. Thus, although monozygotic co-twins have identical thresholds, it is other factors (collectively described as 'stress') that determine whether neither, one, or both eventually develop the disease.

Another approach to examining nature-versus-nurture or genes-versus-environment hypotheses involves the study of persons who are adopted at birth and reared by persons who are not genetic relatives. Several different strategies have been used. One method starts with parents known to have schizophrenia whose offspring were reared by 'normal' adoptive parents. Another starts with adoptees known to have schizophrenia and looks for the disease in the families of their biologic and adoptive relatives.

Both types of 'cross-fostering' studies provide additional evidence for genetic transmission of vulnerability. They also examine whether being raised by a parent who has schizophrenia (ie, who provides a putative 'schizophrenogenic' family environment) contributes to the subsequent development of schizophrenia by the adoptee. So far, support for this hypothesis is unimpressive.

Mechanism of Genetic Transmission

It has long been agreed that observed familial patterns of schizophrenia do not fit any single-gene pattern of Mendelian transmission. Possibilities that might explain the data include the following: (1) genetic heterogeneity, in which several (perhaps many) distinct single-gene mechanisms each occur in a subset of cases; (2) additive or multiplicative interactions among a small number of major genes; (3) polygenic transmission involving many minor genes interacting additively (quantitative trait loci, or QTLs); and (4) the existence of nongenetic forms of the disorder. The most complex possibility, of course, is that each of these theories is correct for some proportion of cases. Gottesman refers to the latter as the "ecumenical" or "combined" model and notes that there is no way it can be decisively refuted.

So far, linkage or association studies have reported data suggesting that genes of major effect may exist on chromosomes 3, 5, 6, 8, and 22, but most of these findings have failed confirmation by independent replication.

Other Risk Factors for Schizophrenia

Many authors have reported associations between pregnancy and birth complications (collectively referred to as *obstetrical complications*) and a subsequent risk for schizophrenia. The most frequent interpretation is that obstetrical complications interact with the genetically determined vulnerability and may not be risk factors for schizophrenia in the absence of the latter.

Frequent findings include associations with low birth weight, prematurity, preeclampsia, and many different complications of labor and delivery. For the latter, reported associations are generally low in magnitude, but studies using weighted summary scores provide evidence that neonatal hypoxia may be the common denominator. For example, studies of monozygotic twins discordant for schizophrenia find that, compared with their healthy co-twins, the affected co-twins have total scores for obstetrical complications two to four times greater and are more likely to show structural brain abnormalities, such as enlargement of the lateral ventricles. When both twins are affected, the scores are higher and brain abnormalities more frequent for the twin with more severe illness.

Jones and Cannon reviewed studies of prenatal, perinatal, and developmental risk factors for schizophrenia.

Table 2-3: Obstetrical Risk Factors for Schizophrenia

Risk Factor	Approximate Relative Risk
Preeclampsia	9
Perinatal brain damage	7
Rhesus incompatibility	3
Severe maternal mal-nutrition in first trimester	2
Exposure to influenza in second trimester	2
Birth during winter or early spring months	1.1

Modified from Jones P, Cannon M: The new epidemiology of schizophrenia. *Psychiatr Clin North Am* 1998;21:1-25.

Their conclusions about some of these risks are summarized in Table 2-3.

Many studies have reported that persons born during the winter or early spring months, especially in the northern hemisphere, have greater risk for subsequent development of schizophrenia than persons born at other times. The magnitude of the increase is modest, about 10%. Warner and de Girolamo tabulated 14 studies from the northern hemisphere and 2 from the southern hemisphere, each involving a minimum of 2,000 subjects, and they concluded that the finding requires explanation. Excluding artifacts, some of the possibilities are: (1) a seasonal variation in the risk of premature delivery or other birth complications; (2) increased spring and summer mating of parents of persons with schizophrenia; (3) maternal nutritional factors related to season or temperature; (4) effects of influenza or other seasonal infectious diseases during pregnancy; and (5) some genetic advantage, associated with vulnerability to schizophrenia, that increases the chances of surviving certain intrauterine risks during cold weather. The last is called the *genetic gain hypothesis.*

Patients with schizophrenia, compared with control groups, have increased scores on scales measuring minor physical anomalies, such as peculiarities in shape of fingers and hands, abnormal dermatoglyphics, and malformations in palatal and other oral structures. Another frequent finding is an increased rate of neurologic 'soft signs.' Retrospective studies find increased rates of small head circumference at birth, delayed developmental milestones, closed head trauma before 3 years of age, and increased clumsiness and speech abnormalities during childhood. These findings are discussed further in Chapter 6.

The Schizophrenia Spectrum of Psychopathology

The familial pattern described above is not specific for schizophrenia but encompasses several other disorders with similar clinical features. The concept of 'schizophrenia spectrum disease' includes not only schizophrenia, but also schizophreniform disorder, schizoaffective disorder, and schizotypal and paranoid personality disorders. Schizoid personality disorder may also be included, but this is less certain. These conditions are believed to share genetic predisposition with schizophrenia and to represent less severe expressions (in the personality disorders) or the presence of additional vulnerabilities (eg, diathesis for mood disorder).

Some studies also find increased rates of mood disorders and a tendency for mood disorders to occur in psychotic form among relatives of persons with schizophrenia. Rates of alcoholism and anxiety disorders, however, do not seem to be increased. This suggests a degree of specificity rather than a general increase in all forms of psychopathology.

Suggested Readings

Barbato A: *Schizophrenia and Public Health.* Geneva, World Health Organization, 1996.

Gottesman II: *Schizophrenia Genesis: The Origins of Madness.* New York, WH Freeman and Company, 1991.

Jablensky A: The 100-year epidemiology of schizophrenia. *Schizophr Res* 1997;28:111-125.

Johnstone EC, Humphreys MS, Lang FH, et al: *Schizophrenia: Concepts and Clinical Management.* Cambridge, Cambridge University Press, 1999.

Jones P, Cannon M: The new epidemiology of schizophrenia. *Psychiatr Clin North Am* 1998;21:1-25.

Schwartzkopf SB, Nasrallah HA, Olson SC, et al: Perinatal complications and genetic loading in schizophrenia: preliminary findings. *Psychiatry Res* 1989;27:233-239.

Tsuang MT, Tohen M, Zahner GP: *Textbook in Psychiatric Epidemiology.* New York, John Wiley & Sons, 1995.

Warner R, de Girolamo G: *Epidemiology of Mental Disorders and Psychosocial Problems: Schizophrenia.* Geneva, World Health Organization, 1995.

Wilcox JA, Nasrallah HA: Perinatal insult as a risk factor in paranoid and nonparanoid schizophrenia. *Psychopathology* 1987; 20:285-287.

Chapter 3

Diagnosis and Subtypes of Schizophrenia

Diagnosis is the linchpin of scientific medicine. The diagnosis of a patient's condition concisely summarizes important clinical findings, communicates those findings unambiguously, and grants the patient access to the sick role. Most importantly, a valid diagnosis connects the patient's condition with the pertinent body of scientific knowledge. It carries an implied prediction about the clinical outcome and the likely costs, efficacy, benefits, and disadvantages of various treatment modalities. Regardless of its efficacy, a treatment cannot be used to maximum advantage without a diagnostic process that has adequate reliability and validity.

During the 1970s, international studies by the World Health Organization and other agencies verified that schizophrenia was diagnosed more frequently in the United States than in other countries. The studies also demonstrated that the likely explanation for the discrepancy was the use of more permissive diagnostic standards by US psychiatrists. Clinicians from most other countries showed close agreement on the clinical features leading to the diagnosis.

Efforts to achieve consensus among US psychiatrists led to the development of standardized evaluation procedures and operational diagnostic criteria. Publication of the third edition of the *Diagnostic and Statistical Manual of Mental Disorders* (DSM-III) in 1980 committed organized psychia-

Table 3-1: Summary of DSM-IV Criteria for Diagnosis of Schizophrenia

A. Symptoms characteristic of the active phase include any one of Schneider's first-rank signs (see Table 1-2), any bizarre delusion, or at least two of the following:

(1) a nonbizarre delusion

(2) a non-Schneiderian hallucination

(3) seriously disorganized speech, such as frequent derailment or incoherence

(4) behavior that is grossly disorganized or catatonic

(5) one or more 'negative' symptoms: affective flattening, alogia, or avolition

B. Significant decline in personal, social, or occupational functioning

C. A period of illness continuous for at least 6 months, either currently or at some time in the past. This period must include at least 1 month of active (psychotic)-phase symptoms as specified above. The remainder of the period may include prodromal and residual phases, which precede and follow the active phase, and during which symptoms are evident but of less than psychotic intensity (ie, the person is not grossly out of contact with external reality).

try to standardization and shifted debate on diagnosis from theoretical to empirical issues. Today, most psychiatrists in the United States diagnose schizophrenia according to the recommendations of DSM-IV; most psychiatrists in other countries follow either DSM-IV or the *International Classification of Diseases*, Revision 10 (ICD-10).

DSM-IV uses the method of *syndromal diagnosis* that is commonly used by all physicians, except in the most technically advanced subspecialities. It defines psychiat-

D. Exclude schizoaffective disorder and mood disorders. Do not diagnose schizophrenia if the clinical features meet criteria for a major depressive episode, manic episode, or mixed episode for a substantial portion of the time during which criteria for schizophrenia are met. (A depressive episode may be superimposed on schizophrenia and diagnosed as a second condition, provided it is present for a relatively small portion of the duration of the episode of schizophrenia.)

E. Exclude general medical conditions and substance-induced conditions. Do not diagnose schizophrenia if the clinical features are caused by the direct physiologic effects of a general medical condition that is present, or substance use, or substance withdrawal.

F. Distinguish from pervasive developmental disorders. Do not diagnose schizophrenia in a person who has previously met criteria for autistic disorder or another pervasive developmental disorder unless the person has delusions or hallucinations (which are not seen in the pervasive developmental disorders).

ric syndromes by *inclusion criteria* based on observable clinical features and then guides the differential diagnosis by means of *exclusion criteria* specifying which diagnosis takes precedence when features overlapping more than one condition are present. The Mental and Behavioural Disorders chapter of ICD-10 likewise provides criteria recommended for research. The ICD-10 research criteria for schizophrenia are similar to those of DSM-IV, although several significant differences will be mentioned later.

DSM-IV criteria for schizophrenia are summarized in Table 3-1. No symptom is pathognomonic of schizophrenia (or any other diagnosis) in DSM-IV, and, with the debatable exception of abnormalities of consciousness, any psychiatric symptom may be present in schizophrenia. The criteria focus on a group of common symptoms that are considered most characteristic of schizophrenia.

The differential diagnosis of schizophrenia, based on exclusion criteria of DSM-IV (D, E, and F in Table 3-1), will be examined in the next chapter. This chapter will focus on inclusion criteria.

Criterion A: Characteristic Symptoms

Criterion A in Table 3-1 specifies the symptoms that define the *active* phase of schizophrenia, when the person is grossly out of contact with reality (ie, is 'actively' psychotic).

The active phase may be preceded and followed by *prodromal* and *residual* phases (Figure 3-1). During these phases, the person either shows a clear decline in function (prodromal) or fails to return to the previous level of function following an active phase (residual), and has attenuated clinical features similar to those in criterion A—that is, symptoms are evident but are not severe enough to cause major loss of contact with reality. Examples of such symptoms include social isolation or withdrawal; peculiar behavior (such as hoarding garbage or talking to oneself in public); blunted, flat, or inappropriate affect; digressive, vague, or stilted speech; unusual perceptual experiences that are not hallucinations (such as frequent misinterpretation of actual perceptual stimuli, or 'sensing' the presence of a person not actually present, without actually seeing or hearing that person); and odd or bizarre ideas that are not delusional (eg, overvalued ideas, ideas of reference, unusual superstitions, feelings of special abilities).

The five groups of symptoms listed by criterion A for the active phase of schizophrenia are defined and described below.

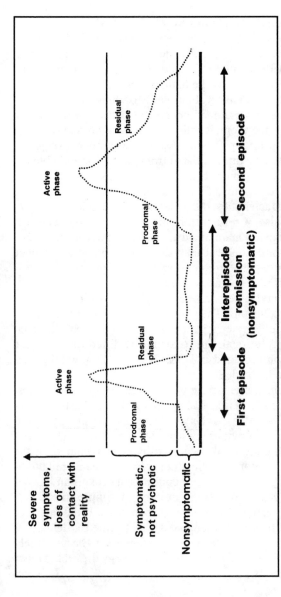

Figure 3-1: Phases of illness in schizophrenia. At least one episode must have an active phase lasting at least 1 month and a total duration (including prodromal, active, and residual phases) of at least 6 months.

43

Criterion A (1): Delusions

Delusions, loosely defined as false beliefs that are incorrigibly maintained despite logical argument and contrary evidence that most people would find convincing, are often viewed as the hallmark of madness. By definition, a delusion is an abnormality of thought content representing a gross impairment of contact with reality; a true delusion, therefore, is pathognomonic of psychosis but not of any specific psychotic disorder. For this reason, delusions must be differentiated from false or improbable beliefs that have more benign explanations.

Most definitions describe a delusional belief as having four characteristics: the belief is idiosyncratic, it is objectively false, it results from incorrect reasoning, and it is intransigently maintained against all efforts at correction. In fact, philosophical analysis and experimental evidence demonstrate that problems arise when applying this definition. It may be impossible to state any definition or procedure having perfect sensitivity and specificity for identifying delusions. The working clinician, however, needs to decide whether a patient's statements should be considered delusional. The following modified version of the definition provided in DSM-IV suggests how this decision can be made:

A delusion is a false belief, based on incorrect inference about external reality, that is firmly sustained despite what everyone else believes, and despite incontrovertible and obvious evidence to the contrary. The belief is not one ordinarily accepted by other members of the person's culture or subculture or by people of similar ethnic, religious, political, or educational background. A delusion is not merely an opinion, a simple mistake, a memory error, or a common superstition. If the false belief involves a value judgment, it is regarded as delusional only when the judgment is so extreme as to be absolutely incredible. (See Table 3-2 for terminology describing types of delusions.)

Delusions must be distinguished from several other types of abnormal thoughts. An *obsession* is a persistently and frequently recurrent thought, impulse, idea, or mental image that is experienced as intrusive, unwanted, and (usually) senseless and distressing (eg, frequent urges to shout out obscenities while in church). The most common obsessions include recurrent fears of contamination; doubts about one's actions (eg, whether the stove was turned off before leaving home); intense needs for objects to be arranged in a particular order or for events to occur in a particular manner; and thoughts of performing aggressive, disgusting, embarrassing, or horrifying actions that are clearly contrary to the person's wishes or standards. The critical characteristic that distinguishes an obsession from a delusion is that the person recognizes the thought as senseless and incorrect. Obsessions may occur in any phase of schizophrenia. They are not useful for making the diagnosis, but Eugen Bleuler observed that obsessions may occasionally transform into delusions.

An *overvalued idea* is an unreasonable and sustained belief similar to a delusion, except that it is accepted with less conviction (ie, the person is able to accept the possibility that the belief might not be true). A common form of overvalued idea is an *idea of reference*, in which a person thinks that someone else's behavior or a neutral event has special meaning for the person. Overvalued ideas are common in all phases of schizophrenia but are also seen in other psychiatric disorders and sometimes in situations not considered psychopathologic.

A *partial delusion* is an overvalued idea that involves content so bizarre or inexplicable that it seems abnormal to entertain the idea at all. Although not recognized by DSM-IV, partial delusions are considered by some clinicians to have the same diagnostic value as full delusions.

Criterion A (2): Hallucinations

A hallucination is a perceptual experience that has a compelling sense of reality, like a true perception, but it

Table 3-2: Types of Delusions

• *Bizarre delusion:* one involving a belief that persons similar to the patient regard as totally incredible (eg, that the earth is changing into a reptile).

• *Crystallized delusion:* one in which the details are fully elaborated and remain constant over time.

• *Delusional jealousy:* that the person's spouse or significant other (sexual partner) is unfaithful.

• *Delusion of being controlled (of passivity):* that the person's thoughts, feelings, impulses, or actions are somehow controlled externally rather than being under personal control.

• *Delusion of reference:* that actions of other persons, or neutral objects or events, have a special meaning for (ie, refer to) the person (eg, that other persons are smiling because they want him or her to die). Distinguished from *idea of reference*, in which such a belief is held with less than delusional conviction or persistence. Ideas of reference are far more common than delusions of reference and are not diagnostic of psychosis.

• *Depressive delusions:* delusions involving themes of extreme personal inadequacy, guilt, disease, death, nihilism, or deserved punishment. Although considered more typical of depressive disorders, delusions of these types can be seen in schizophrenia.

(Note: also see Table 1-2.)

occurs without external stimulation of the sensory organ. A person may or may not have insight into the nonreality of a hallucination. Transient hallucinations may occur in nonpsychotic mental disorders and in some situations (eg, acute bereavement) that are not considered psychopathologic. In certain cultures, particular hallucinatory experiences are considered normal, expected,

- **Encapsulated delusion:** a delusional belief involving a relatively restricted and circumscribed topic (eg, a single person or idea) in a person whose thought and behavior are otherwise normal.
- **Erotomanic delusion:** that another individual, usually someone of higher social status or prestige (eg, an entertainer, athlete, politician), or an individual especially respected by the person (eg, a priest, doctor, teacher), is in love with the person.
- **Grandiose delusion:** that the person has extraordinary worth, power, or knowledge or a special relationship to a deity or a famous or important person (eg, that God has given the person a divine mandate to establish a new government).
- **Nihilistic delusion:** that the person, part of the person's body, the universe, or an important part of the universe does not exist or has ceased to exist.
- **Persecutory delusion:** that the person is or has been attacked, harassed, cheated, injured, threatened, or conspired against by others (eg, that food is being poisoned).
- **Somatic delusion (hypochondriacal delusion):** that some feature of the appearance, structure, or function of the person's body is abnormal or has changed (eg, that parasites are destroying internal organs).
- **Systematized delusions:** a group of delusional beliefs that are logically interconnected.

and desirable. For example, they may have religious, developmental, or communal importance. Hallucinations that serve an understandable cultural function should be considered nonpathologic. The term is not applied to dreaming during sleep or to neurologic symptoms such as tinnitus. Terminology describing hallucinations is defined in Table 3-3.

Table 3-3: Types of Hallucinations

• *Auditory hallucination:* involving the perception of sound, often of human voices. This is the most frequent type of hallucination in schizophrenia and mood disorders. Hallucinations in other sensory modalities without any auditory hallucinations strongly suggest a secondary mental disorder (ie, caused by the direct physiologic effects of a general medical condition, substance use, or substance withdrawal).

• *Command hallucination:* a voice commanding the person to perform some action, sometimes dangerous or violent. Patients may be greatly troubled by command hallucinations and sometimes act as a result of them.

• *Extracampine hallucination:* one perceived as coming from a location beyond the range of normal perception.

• *Gustatory hallucination:* involving the perception of taste (usually unpleasant).

• *Kinesthetic hallucination:* involving feelings of movement.

• *Olfactory hallucination:* involving the perception of odor, usually foul (eg, burnt rubber).

• *Schneiderian hallucination:* an auditory hallucination of a voice speaking the person's thoughts aloud or

(Note: also see Table 1-2.)

Auditory hallucinations of voices are among the most common symptoms of schizophrenia. They may be fleeting or recurrent, or they may continue for years. Patients are often disturbed or puzzled by them, and some are overwhelmed and tormented by them. Sometimes patients may become indifferent toward hallucinated voices or acquire partial insight into their unreality, while still experiencing them involuntarily. Patients sometimes can learn to ignore or suppress hallucinations (eg, by humming). Awareness commenting on them, or describing or commenting on the person's activities as they occur, or of two or more voices arguing or discussing the person.

• *Somatic hallucination:* involving a sensation localized inside the body (such as a feeling of electricity in the head or of snakes in the intestine). Often, the sensation is one that is physiologically impossible. Somatic hallucinations must be distinguished from true sensations (eg, arising from an as-yet-undiagnosed general medical condition), from hypochondriacal preoccupation with normal internal sensations (eg, one's heartbeat or peristalsis), and from tactile hallucinations.

• *Tactile (haptic) hallucination:* involving the sensation of touch on or immediately beneath the skin. The most common tactile hallucinations involve feelings of insects or other creatures crawling; this symptom is called *formication.*

• *Visual hallucination:* involving the sense of sight. Visual hallucinations may consist of unformed images (eg, flashes of light), simple formed images (eg, visions of people), or complex formed images (eg, apocalyptic imagery or people acting in a real-seeming but non-existent environment).

that other people do not experience these perceptions may be present or absent.

The content of auditory hallucinations varies from indistinct muttering to elaborate conversations involving several parties. The source may seem unlocatable, or it may be perceived as coming from all around, from a particular point in the environment, or from inside the head or another body part. The voices may be familiar or unfamiliar. Commonly, the language is coarse, hostile, insulting, belittling, or derogatory, but it also may be comforting, praising, instructing, or neutral. Except in the case of audible thoughts (see Table 1-2), references to the patient are usually in the second or third person.

Hallucinations are distinguished from *illusions*, in which a genuine sensory stimulus is interpreted or recognized incorrectly (eg, the rustling of leaves is thought to be persons whispering). Illusions often accompany true hallucinations and are frequent in the prodromal and residual phases of schizophrenia. They can also occur under conditions in which sensory discrimination is difficult, or when the person is fatigued, inattentive, apprehensive, excessively vigilant, or simply mistaken.

Other perceptual distortions associated with schizophrenia involve alterations in the apparent size, shape, distance, color, or brightness of objects seen or in the quality, timbre, melody, duration, emotional content, or familiarity of sounds heard. Such abnormalities may be experienced in any sensory modality and may occur at any stage of schizophrenia. They also occur in many other psychopathologic or nonpathologic states.

Criterion A (3): Disorganized Speech

The term *thought disorder* (sometimes more fully termed *formal thought disorder* or *thought process disorder*) refers to abnormalities in the form, structure, organization, sequencing, progression, or speed of thinking rather than in the content of thoughts. Because it is not possible to directly perceive a patient's thinking processes, the clinician must recognize the symptoms of thought disorder based on the person's speech. Common types of thinking and speech disorders are defined in Table 3-4.

Although some clinicians and researchers believe that formal thought disorder is the single abnormality most characteristic of schizophrenia, none of the symptoms of formal thought disorder is specific to this diagnosis. Mild disorganization of speech is common in a wide range of pathologic and nonpathologic circumstances. When disorganized speech is counted as a criterion to diagnose the active phase of schizophrenia, it should be included only if the disorganization is so severe as to substantially impair communication. Less severe impairment is seen in the prodromal and residual phases of schizophrenia.

Criterion A (4): Grossly Disorganized or Catatonic Behavior

Grossly disorganized behavior encompasses a wide range of abnormalities and should be counted toward diagnosis of schizophrenia only when the behavioral abnormalities are severe and clearly seem to be evidence of illness. "For example," DSM-IV states, "a few instances of restless, angry, or agitated behavior should not be considered to be evidence of schizophrenia, especially if the motivation is understandable."

Examples of grossly disorganized behavior might include prolonged childlike silliness; severe agitation (excessive motor activity accompanied by intense affect); inability to satisfactorily complete normal goal-directed behaviors (eg, activities of daily living or personal hygiene); displays of affect markedly inappropriate to circumstances (eg, grinning while discussing a tragic event); intense verbal or physical aggressiveness that is unpredictable and unprovoked; serious loss of normal social inhibitions (eg, public masturbation); and other actions that seem so odd or unusual that they suggest the person is grossly out of contact with external reality.

Catatonia is a syndrome of abnormally increased muscle tone and decreased responsiveness, usually resulting in stuporous immobility but occasionally resulting in frenzied or excited motor activity. Precise usage of the term would restrict the concept to persons who are neurophysiologically alert, but in common usage this distinction may be overlooked. The symptoms usually considered to be evidence of catatonia are listed in Table 3-5.

Because Kraepelin included this distinctive syndrome as one of the core subtypes of dementia praecox, clinicians

Table 3-4: Abnormalities of Thinking and Speech

Abnormalities of Associative Thinking

• *Loose associations:* the general term for shifts in train of thought or speech that occur without adequate logical connection. Normal progression of goal-directed thinking may be described as *tight associations.* Looseness or tightness are variable in degree; loose associations are an occasional experience in normal mental life.

• *Clang associations:* shifts in thought related to sounds rather than meanings of words.

• *Derailment:* a tendency for thought to be easily deflected to a different topic, or to 'run off the track.' Also called *knight's-move thinking.*

• *Flight of ideas:* abnormally rapid progression of thoughts with many abrupt shifts in topic that are usually based on understandable loose associations, distracting stimuli, or plays on words; often accompanied by *pressured speech,* which is intense, rapid, often loud, and difficult to interrupt, as if the person feels compelled to keep talking.

• *Verbigeration:* despite adequate quantity, speech conveys little or no information because of excessive vagueness, useless repetitions, meaningless or clichéd phrases, etc.

• *Word salad:* associations so loose that speech is incoherent.

Abnormalities of Thought Progression and Goal-Directedness

• *Blocking:* sudden, involuntary, complete interruption in progress of speech or thought.

• *Circumstantiality:* a tendency to digress and to insert irrelevant information and unnecessary explanations and qualifications before a thought is eventually completed.

Abnormalities of Thought Progression and Goal-Directedness *(continued)*

• *Perseveration:* repetition or persistence of a thought when it is no longer appropriate; inability to make appropriate shifts in thinking.

• *Racing thoughts:* thoughts are experienced as progressing out of control more rapidly than they can be spoken.

• *Tangentiality:* digression and irrelevancy so severe that the intended goal is never reached.

Abnormalities of Grammar and Vocabulary

• *Mannerism:* an odd or eccentric expression, especially if used recurrently.

• *Neologism:* a new word or phrase that seems to have a private or special meaning and whose derivation is not readily apparent.

• *Paraphasia:* use of erroneous words that are phonetically or semantically related to the target word.

• *Stereotypy:* frequent, mechanical repetition of a word or phrase, always or sometimes without apparent purpose; may seem automatic, even involuntary.

• *Word approximation:* idiosyncratic word usage that seems stilted or peculiar but whose meaning is evident.

(continued on next page)

Table 3-4: Abnormalities of Thinking and Speech *(continued)*

Abnormalities of Logic, Reasoning, or Perspective of Thought

• *Concrete thinking:* excessive literalness of expression and narrowness of understanding; inability to think beyond the context of the immediate present, to generalize, to recognize any meaning but the most overt, and to appreciate symbolism and metaphor.

• *Non sequitur:* reasoning in which the conclusion is not logically supported by the premises.

• *Overinclusive thinking:* inability to maintain conceptual boundaries, so that irrelevant or distantly associated elements become incorporated into concepts, making thought less precise, less understandable, and often more abstract.

• *Talking past the point (approximate answers, Ganserism):* the person answers questions incorrectly, but in a manner that suggests that the incorrectness is intentional and that the correct answer may be known.

Other Abnormalities of Coherence

• *Driveling:* speech that is copious but meaningless.

• *Poverty of content of speech (wooliness of thought):* despite adequate amount of speech, little information is contained. Statements are vague or excessively abstract or concrete.

once considered catatonic symptoms to be virtually pathognomonic of schizophrenia. Careful research, however, has established that catatonia is more often part of a mood disorder than of schizophrenia. Other psychiatric diagnoses that may include symptoms resembling catatonia include conversion disorders, dissociative disorders, and factitious disorders. Catatonia may also be caused by

Table 3-5: Symptoms of Catatonia

• *Automatic obedience:* the person complies with commands in a robot-like manner, apparently without critical judgment.

• *Catalepsy:* generalized immobility with markedly diminished responsiveness to stimuli despite normal consciousness; also called *catatonic stupor.*

• *Catatonic excitement:* severe, apparently purposeless hyperactivity not influenced by external stimuli.

• *Catatonic mutism:* inability to speak in a patient who has catalepsy.

• *Catatonic negativism:* apparently involuntary or purposeless resistance to instructions, or rigid maintenance of posture against attempts to be moved.

• *Catatonic posturing:* prolonged involuntary maintenance of fixed posture, even if awkward.

• *Catatonic rigidity:* refers to catatonic posturing, negativism, or waxy flexibility.

• *Echolalia:* morbid, parrot-like repetition of another person's speech; often seems automatic and involuntary.

• *Echopraxia:* morbid, stereotyped, automatic mimicking of another person's movements and posture; often seems automatic and involuntary.

• *Stereotypy:* frequent mechanical repetition of speech or a pattern of motor activity, always or sometimes without apparent purpose.

• *Waxy flexibility (cerea flexibilitas):* passive resistance to movement, followed by prolonged maintenance (at least several minutes) of whatever posture one is placed in.

general medical conditions (the DSM-IV term for nonpsychiatric conditions), particularly neurologic disorders involving pathology of the basal ganglia (eg, parkinsonism, Huntington's disease, or progressive supranuclear palsy) and seizure disorders (eg, petit mal or complex partial seizures).

Criterion A (5): Negative Symptoms

The division of symptoms into positive and negative categories was evidently first suggested by a neurologist named Reynolds in 1857. Positive symptoms, such as spasms and convulsions, reflected the 'excess or alteration of vital properties,' while negative symptoms, such as paralysis and anesthesia, were those that represented a 'negation of the vital properties.' Somewhat later, Hughlings Jackson classified losses of function caused by a presumed anatomic lesion as negative symptoms, while positive symptoms resulted from excesses of normal functioning that had lost inhibitory regulation as a result of that lesion.

The terms are used in a similar manner today. Positive symptoms are presumed to result from an excess or distortion of some normal neurophysiologic function, while negative symptoms reflect a loss or diminution of normal function. Examples of positive symptoms include those listed in criteria A (1), A (2), and A (4). Symptoms in criterion A (3) are often grouped in a third category, disorganization of thought; blocking and poverty of content of thought are sometimes considered negative symptoms.

Symptoms generally included in the negative category are listed in Table 3-6. Note, however, that criterion A (5) mentions only affective flattening, alogia, and avolition as criteria for the diagnosis of schizophrenia.

Difficulties can arise in evaluating negative symptoms. First, these symptoms tend to occur on a continuum, without clear cutoffs between normality and abnormality. Second, it is necessary to distinguish between *primary* negative symptoms that represent a true loss of function resulting from a disease process, and *secondary* negative

Table 3-6: Negative Symptoms

• *Affective flattening or blunting:* reduction or absence of external signs of emotion. Includes generalized lack of responsiveness, immobile and unresponsive facial expression, decreased spontaneous movements, paucity of expressive gestures, poor eye contact, and lack of vocal inflection.

• *Alogia:* a reduction in quantity of thought, which is reflected in decreased fluency and productivity of speech; not simply an unwillingness to talk. Alogia includes *poverty of speech* (ie, reduction in amount, with verbalizations tending to be brief, concrete, and unelaborated); *poverty of content of speech* (speech is adequate in amount but is excessively vague, concrete, or generalized, conveying little information); *blocking* (interruptions in the train of thought); and *prolonged response latencies* (long pauses before initiating responses).

• *Anhedonia:* loss or reduction in capacity for experiencing pleasure, as may be manifested by lack of interest in enjoyable activities, or a decrease in sexual interest, activity, or enjoyment.

• *Asociality:* reduction or absence of interest in relationships and interactions with other persons, including inability to feel intimacy and closeness.

• *Avolition (apathy):* reduction or loss of ability to initiate and persist in goal-directed activities. Typically includes poor grooming, impersistence at work or school, and physical anergia.

• *Inattentiveness:* inability to maintain task involvement or engagement for a reasonable period of time.

Modified from Andreasen N: The scale for the assessment of negative symptoms (SANS). Iowa City, University of Iowa, 1981.

symptoms that may be explainable as medication side effects, lack of environmental stimulation, discouragement, or depression. Negative symptoms can also occur secondary to positive symptoms. For example, a very suspicious patient may become asocial, or a patient who has the delusion that speech will cause the end of the world may seem to manifest alogia. Although the distinction can be difficult to make in clinical practice, criterion A (5) refers to primary negative symptoms.

Criterion B: Decline in Functioning

This criterion, which is not included in ICD-10, requires a significant period of time in which a person's functioning in social, academic, occupational, or self-care activities is significantly below a previously demonstrated level. If symptom onset is in childhood or adolescence, the criterion may be met by failure to achieve normal levels expected for age and previous developmental trajectory.

Criterion C: Duration

The duration requirement is the most significant difference between ICD-10 criteria and DSM-IV criteria. ICD-10 requires a period of at least 1 month in which criterion A symptoms are prominent (ie, an active phase lasting at least 1 month).

DSM-IV requires that, at least once during a person's life, an active phase lasting at least 1 month ("or shorter if successfully treated") be embedded within a 6-month period during which signs of the illness are continuously present (see Figure 3-1). The 6-month period may include a prodromal phase preceding the active phase and a residual phase following the active phase. After this initial 6-month period, there are no duration requirements for subsequent episodes of illness to be considered recurrences of schizophrenia.

This criterion serves to incorporate a longitudinal (Kraepelinian) perspective into the diagnosis. It is sometimes criticized as leading to a self-fulfilling prophecy, because chronicity is required for the diagnosis rather than merely being an observed feature of the condition.

Other Common Features of Schizophrenia

Criterion A identifies a relatively small group of symptoms considered to be sufficient to diagnose the active phase of schizophrenia. Many other symptoms are also seen, but they are considered less discriminating.

Any abnormality of affect may occur in schizophrenia. *Dysphoric symptoms* such as depression, anxiety, anger, irritability, and hostility occur more frequently than signs of elevated mood such as grandiosity, elation, and expansiveness. When full criteria are met for a major depressive or manic episode, the diagnosis will most often be a mood disorder with psychotic features or schizoaffective disorder rather than schizophrenia. This issue will be discussed in the next chapter.

Neurovegetative symptoms such as disturbed sleep and loss of energy occur in some patients. Refusal of food is likely to result from delusional beliefs, such as a fear of being poisoned.

Abnormalities of motor activity may include psychomotor retardation and various forms of restlessness such as pacing, rocking, hypermotility, and agitation. Other abnormal movements may include grimacing, stereotypies (repetitive, irrational, nonproductive motor activities), odd mannerisms, grunting, and ritualistic behavior. There may also be involuntary adventitious movements such as twitches, chorea, or athetosis. These symptoms may, of course, be medication side effects, but movement abnormalities had been observed in some patients long before the discovery of neuroleptic drugs.

Assaultive and violent behaviors may be shown by a minority of patients, notably by younger men with a past history of violence. Noncompliance with medication and substance abuse also frequently characterize violent patients. As a group, however, people with schizophrenia are no more violent or dangerous than people with other diagnoses or no psychiatric diagnosis at all. Most patients with schizophrenia are more likely to be victims than perpetrators of violent acts.

Poor insight (lack of awareness of having a psychotic illness) is present in almost every patient with schizophrenia. It is associated with poor compliance with treatment, frequent relapses into the active phase, and involuntary hospitalizations, as well as a variety of other psychosocial consequences such as frequent arrests and homelessness.

Patients with schizophrenia are at increased risk for many forms of substance abuse. It is estimated that more than 80% of persons with schizophrenia are heavy cigarette smokers. Other drugs frequently abused include alcohol, cannabis, anticholinergics, and 'activating' drugs such as sympathomimetics.

Clinical features such as soft neurologic signs, neuropsychologic deficits, and psychophysiologic abnormalities will be described in Chapter 6.

Subtypes of Schizophrenia in DSM-IV and ICD-10

Despite widespread agreement that schizophrenia is a heterogeneous group of conditions, there is little consensus on defining homogeneous subtypes. DSM-IV and ICD-10 follow the traditional (Kraepelinian) approach of describing subtypes according to cross-sectional clinical features. Table 3-7 outlines the criteria for subtypes listed in DSM-IV.

Note that the residual type of schizophrenia is a phase of the illness rather than a true subtype. In the United States, the most frequent subtype is the undifferentiated, followed by the paranoid, disorganized, and catatonic. Catatonia is diagnosed more frequently in many other countries.

ICD-10 lists two additional subtypes: *simple schizophrenia* and *postschizophrenic depressive episode*. DSM-IV does not list these as subtypes of schizophrenia, but it includes both (simple schizophrenia is referred to as *simple deterio-*

Table 3-7: DSM-IV Criteria for Subtypes of Schizophrenia

- *Catatonic type:* The clinical picture is dominated by at least two of the following: (see Table 3-5 for definitions)

  (1) Catalepsy, waxy flexibility, or stupor

  (2) Catatonic excitement

  (3) Extreme negativism or mutism

  (4) Peculiarities of voluntary movements such as posturing, stereotypies, prominent mannerisms, or prominent grimacing

  (5) Echolalia or echopraxia

- *Disorganized (hebephrenic) type:*

  A. All of the following are present:

    (1) disorganized speech

    (2) disorganized behavior

    (3) flat or inappropriate affect

  B. Criteria are not met for the catatonic type (one catatonic symptom may be present).

- *Paranoid type:*

  A. Preoccupation with one or more delusions or frequent auditory hallucinations.

  B. No symptoms listed for the catatonic and disorganized subtypes are prominent.

- *Undifferentiated type:* Symptoms that meet criterion A for schizophrenia are present (see Table 3-1) but do not meet criteria for catatonic, disorganized, or paranoid types.

- *Residual type:*

  A. Delusions, hallucinations, grossly disorganized or catatonic behavior, and severely disorganized speech are not present.

  B. Negative symptoms or attenuated forms of criterion A symptoms are present.

Table 3-8: DSM-IV Criteria for Simple Deteriorative Disorder

Note: DSM-IV includes this condition in its Appendix B, Criteria Sets for Further Study. It corresponds closely with simple schizophrenia, which ICD-10 lists as a subtype of schizophrenia.

A. Progressive development over a period of at least a year of all of the following:

(1) Marked deterioration in functioning

(2) Gradual appearance and worsening of negative symptoms (affective flattening, alogia, and avolition)

(3) Poor interpersonal rapport, social isolation, or social withdrawal

B. The person has never met criterion A for schizophrenia.

C. All of the following must be excluded as adequate explanations for the symptoms listed above: schizotypal and schizoid personality disorders, other psychotic disorders, mood disorders, anxiety disorders, dementia, mental retardation, general medical conditions, substance use, and substance withdrawal.

---

rative disorder) in its Appendix B, Criteria Sets for Further Study. Table 3-8 summarizes the criteria suggested for simple deteriorative disorder. DSM-IV defines postschizophrenic depressive disorder as a "major depressive episode superimposed on the residual phase of schizophrenia."

DSM-II, published in 1968, also listed the following as subtypes of schizophrenia: *acute schizophrenic episode*, *schizoaffective schizophrenia, latent schizophrenia, childhood schizophrenia*, and a residual category, *other schizophrenia*. Under the latter category, some psychiatrists included conditions they called *pseudoneurotic schizo-phrenia, pseudopsychopathic schizophrenia*, and *border-line schizophrenia*.

In DSM-IV, acute schizophrenic episode corresponds roughly with *brief psychotic disorder* or *schizophreniform disorder*, and schizoaffective schizophrenia has become *schizoaffective disorder* (no longer considered a subtype of schizophrenia). These conditions are reviewed in the following chapter.

Childhood schizophrenia has been deleted as a sepa-rate diagnostic category, and most of the conditions that would have been categorized here in DSM-II are now clas-sified as *pervasive developmental disorders*. True schizo-phrenia rarely begins before puberty and is not diagnosed as a separate subtype when it does.

Latent schizophrenia was a nebulous category based on Bleuler's terminology. Today, some of these patients would be diagnosed as having schizotypal or schizoid personality disorder or some other personality or anxiety disorder. Others might not meet criteria for any diagnosis in DSM-IV. The same also applies to pseudoneurotic, pseudopsychopathic, and borderline schizophrenia.

Other Approaches to Patient-Oriented Subtypes of Schizophrenia

During the 1930s, the Norwegian psychiatrist Gabriel Langfeldt suggested a distinction between a core group of *process* or *nuclear* schizophrenias versus a group of *reac-tive* or *peripheral* schizophrenias. Although not referred to in DSM-IV or ICD-10, the process-reactive dichotomy for schizophrenias has clinical and empirical usefulness.

Langfeldt suggested that characteristics of process schizophrenia included poor functioning before the onset of psychosis; a slow, insidious onset of psychosis; onset during adolescence; absence of precipitating events be-fore becoming psychotic; little or no reactivity to life events or changes in the environment; poor recovery from

Table 3-9: Predictors of General Prognosis in Schizophrenia

'Good' Prognosis

- Acute onset of psychosis
- Stress related to onset of psychosis
- Short duration of psychotic symptoms
- Full recovery between episodes
- No prior psychiatric history
- Depression, anxiety, or 'responsive' affect
- Confusion or perplexity while psychotic
- Absence of obsessive-compulsive symptoms
- Absence of assaultive behavior
- Good work (academic, occupational) history
- Higher educational achievement
- Stable marriage
- Older age at onset
- Normal neurologic function
- Normal neuropsychologic function and IQ
- Absence of structural brain abnormalities
- Higher socioeconomic status
- Family history negative for schizophrenia
- Family history positive for mood disorders
- No prominent negative symptoms

episodes; progressive deterioration; and a chronic, deteriorating clinical course. It was presumed to reflect strong hereditary predisposition for psychosis. Process schizophrenia corresponded closely with Kraepelin's original concept of dementia praecox. Some psychiatrists have referred to this as *stainless steel schizophrenia*.

In contrast, reactive schizophrenia was characterized by good functioning before the onset of psychosis; abrupt on-

'Poor' Prognosis
- Insidious onset of psychosis
- No apparent precipitating stress
- Long duration of psychotic symptoms
- Residual symptoms between episodes
- History of previous psychiatric problems
- Flat or inappropriate affect
- No confusion or perplexity while psychotic
- Presence of obsessive-compulsive symptoms
- History of assaultive behavior
- Poor work history
- Lower educational achievement
- Never married
- Onset during adolescence
- Presence of neurologic abnormalities
- Impaired neuropsychologic function, low IQ
- Presence of structural brain abnormalities
- Lower socioeconomic status
- Family history positive for schizophrenia
- Family history negative for mood disorders
- Prominent negative symptoms present

set of psychosis; onset after adolescence; presence of precipitating events at the time of becoming psychotic; reactivity to life events and changes in the environment; good recovery from episodes; absence of deterioration; and a good chance for functional recovery. It was assumed that the person did not have a strong hereditary predisposition and therefore that the psychosis was caused by stressful life events. Reactive schizophrenia corresponded roughly with

Bleuler's broader descriptions of the condition. Some psychiatrists have argued that it might not be schizophrenia at all but rather a severe form of mood disorder.

A similar dichotomization is based on studies that have sought to relate some measure of long-term outcome with various clinical findings. Although 'good prognosis schizophrenia' is often contrasted with 'poor prognosis schizophrenia,' as in Table 3-9, the predictive power of this distinction is modest. One problem is that the terminology is misleading. Outcomes in schizophrenia are multidimensional and variable, so it is an oversimplification to speak of prognosis in the singular form. Also, predictions are reasonably accurate for patients who unequivocally fit into a single category, but most patients have a mixture of characteristics.

Another approach to subclassifying patients with schizophrenia uses various biologic markers, including such features as eye tracking deficits, abnormalities of event-related brain voltage potentials or electrodermal activation, defects in attentional processes such as continuous performance tests, various abnormalities on structural or functional brain imaging procedures, increased nailfold plexus visibility, and decreased platelet monoamine oxidase activity. Combinations of biologic markers are sometimes used to define subgroups of patients in research studies but have no current practical clinical application.

Syndrome-Oriented Subtypes of Schizophrenia

Syndrome-oriented subtyping of schizophrenias attempts to identify distinct subsyndromes of clinical features. These approaches are based on the hypothesis that several distinct pathophysiologic processes operate independently in patients who have schizophrenia, so that many patients show a mixture of several of these processes. (For example, type 2 diabetes mellitus may be a mixture of several pathophysiologic processes operating in the same group of patients.)

Table 3-10: Type I and Type II Subsyndromes in Schizophrenia

Type I Schizophrenia

- Clinical features include delusions, hallucinations, and other positive symptoms
- Tends to occur in acute episodes
- Good response to treatment with typical antipsychotic drugs
- Little or no intellectual impairment
- Absence of irreversible abnormal involuntary movements
- Absence of structural brain abnormalities on in vivo imaging (CT, MRI)
- Hypothesized pathophysiology involves increased density or sensitivity of mesolimbic D_2 receptors

Type II Schizophrenia

- Clinical features include flat affect, alogia, avolition, and other negative symptoms
- Tends to be chronic, often slowly progressive
- Poor response to treatment with typical antipsychotic drugs
- Intellectual impairment may be present
- Presence of irreversible abnormal involuntary movements (spontaneous or drug induced)
- Presence of structural brain abnormalities on in vivo imaging (CT, MRI)
- Hypothesized pathophysiology involves cell loss in temporal and frontal cortex

Two syndrome-oriented approaches have become well known and are invoked in interpretation of various research findings. Crow suggested a two-syndrome model, which is summarized in Table 3-10. Liddle used multivariate statistical methodology to develop a three-syndrome model. He defined the three syndromes as *reality distortion* (consisting mainly of hallucinations and delusions), *disorganization* (formal thought disorder, bizarre behavior, and inappropriate affect), and *psychomotor poverty* (core negative symptoms of poverty of speech, flat or blunted affect, and decreased spontaneous movement).

Suggested Readings

Amador XF, Gorman JM: Psychopathologic domains and insight in schizophrenia. *Psychiatr Clin North Am* 1998;21:27-42.

American Psychiatric Association: *Diagnostic and Statistical Manual of Mental Disorders*, 4th ed. Text Revision (DSM-IV-TR). Washington, DC, American Psychiatric Association, 2000.

Bornstein RA, Nasrallah HA, Olson SC, et al: Neuropsychological deficits in schizophrenic subtypes: comparison of paranoid, nonparanoid and schizoaffective subgroups. *Psychiatry Res* 1990; 31:15-24.

Brekke JS, Prindle C, Bae SW, et al: Risks for individuals with schizophrenia who are living in the community. *Psychiatr Serv* 2001;52:1358-1366.

Crow TJ: Molecular pathology of schizophrenia: more than one disease process? *Br Med J* 1980;280:66-68.

Crow TJ: The two-syndrome concept: origins and current status. *Schizophr Bull* 1985;11:471-486.

Liddle PF: The multidimensional phenotype of schizophrenia. In: Tamminga CA, ed. *Schizophrenia in a Molecular Age.* Washington, DC, American Psychiatric Press; 1999:1-28. Oldham JA, Riba MB, eds. *Review of Psychiatry*; vol 18.

McKenna PJ: *Schizophrenia and Related Syndromes*, 1st ed. Oxford, Oxford University Press, 1994.

Chapter 4

The Differential Diagnosis of Schizophrenia

Advances in treatment efficacy often lead to increases in treatment specificity. When highly specific treatments are available, it is crucial to distinguish accurately among disorders having similar clinical features. Conversely, differential response to specific treatments is a useful criterion for clarifying the boundaries between such conditions.

This chapter lists the standards recommended by the fourth edition of the *Diagnostic and Statistical Manual of Mental Disorders* (DSM-IV) for distinguishing among disorders that have psychotic features similar to the active phase of schizophrenia. Diagnoses that always include psychotic symptoms are grouped by DSM-IV in the same chapter with schizophrenia. Psychotic symptoms may also occur but are not obligatory for the diagnosis in delirium, dementia of the Alzheimer type, and mood disorders. Because psychosis is only a marker of severity and not a distinguishing characteristic of these conditions, they are listed in other chapters of DSM-IV.

Delirium will be examined first, followed by symptomatic psychoses. In these conditions, psychotic symptoms are caused by direct physiologic effects of general medical conditions, substance use, substance withdrawal, or a combination of these. Because their reversibility often depends on accurate identification and effective treatment of the underlying cause(s), it is vitally important that these conditions be ruled out before diagnosing a patient's psychosis as schizophrenia.

Clouded Consciousness and Delirium

Delirium is a polymorphous syndrome resulting from inadequate metabolic support of brain function, caused by the direct physiologic consequences of a general medical condition, substance use, or substance withdrawal. Every clinician should be able to recognize florid delirium, but mild or intermittent delirium is often subtle and may require diagnostic assistance or sensitive cognitive testing.

The diagnostically unique feature of delirium is an *abnormality of consciousness*. Essential components of consciousness include capacity for receiving and responding to stimuli from the environment, degree of clarity of awareness of the environment, accuracy of comprehension of one's circumstances in the environment, and ability to selectively direct and sustain attention.

Any psychiatric abnormality may occur in delirium. Symptoms such as delusional, muddled, confused, or slowed thinking; inarticulate or incoherent speech; psychomotor hyperactivity or hypoactivity; and perceptual aberrations such as hallucinations and illusions are common in both delirium and schizophrenia. Table 4-1 lists some clinical features that have greater discriminatory power for suggesting delirium as a possible cause of psychotic symptoms.

Secondary Psychotic Disorders in Clear Consciousness

The direct physiologic effects of a general medical condition, substance use, or substance withdrawal may also cause psychotic symptoms without any abnormality of consciousness. The patient has normal capacity for attending and responding to the environment and is able to focus

Table 4-1: Clinical Features Suggesting Delirium in a Psychotic Patient

- Altered level of consciousness
- Disorientation for time and place (not caused by delusional thinking)
- Impaired awareness of the environment
- Impaired comprehension of immediate circumstances (not caused by delusional thinking)
- Fluctuations in symptoms or their intensity over a period of hours
- Rapid onset of symptoms
- Recent onset of impairment of memory and other cognitive functions
- Predominance of hallucinations in modalities other than auditory
- Presence of a general medical condition capable of altering metabolic support of brain function
- Evidence of use of a psychoactive substance capable of causing delirium during intoxication or withdrawal

and maintain attention without difficulty. Memory impairment and other cognitive functions are not present or are mild compared with typical delirium and dementia.

When the clinical presentation seems typical of schizophrenia, the possibility of an underlying nonpsychiatric cause may be overlooked. Therefore, many psychiatrists recommend a thorough medical work-up for every new case of schizophrenia. Although this makes sense clinically, ethically, and economically, too often the work-up is abbreviated or neglected because of limited resources or diagnostic carelessness.

Table 4-2 lists some clinical features that suggest that psychotic symptoms in clear consciousness may be caused by a general medical condition or psychoactive substance.

Psychotic Disorders Caused by General Medical Conditions

General medical conditions (a synonym for nonpsychiatric medical conditions) are those listed in the *International Classification of Diseases,* 10th revision (ICD-10) outside of the Mental and Behavioural Disorders chapter. DSM-IV introduced this term when it eliminated the term *organic.* The latter term was considered misleading because it seemed to imply that nonorganic disorders were exclusively nonbiologic in etiology and pathophysiology. As explained in Chapter 6, there are many organic factors associated with schizophrenia that are not general medical conditions.

When a psychotic illness is associated with a general medical condition, it is difficult to decide whether a causal relationship exists. If the association is purely coincidental, or if the general medical condition is partly or completely a consequence of the disturbed behavior, the psychiatric syndrome is a primary psychotic disorder. An inference that the non-psychiatric condition may be causing a secondary psychotic syndrome is usually based on evidence of a pathophysiology that could plausibly alter brain function. The inference is strengthened by features such as parallel fluctuations in clinical course and resolution of the psychosis following effective treatment of the nonpsychiatric condition. Table 4-3 lists many conditions in which these criteria may be met.

Psychotic Disorders Caused by Substance Use or Substance Withdrawal

In DSM-IV, *psychoactive substance* can refer to any drug of abuse, medication, or exogenous toxin that has a direct physiologic effect on mental functioning. Thus, this category includes disorders resulting from intentional substance misuse, from correct or incorrect use of medications for therapeutic purposes, from environmental exposure, and from accidental poisonings.

Table 4-4 lists general categories and examples of substances of these various types that may cause a psychotic syndrome, without delirium, during intoxication or withdrawal.

Psychotic Mood Disorders and Schizoaffective Disorder

Kraepelin's dictum that manic-depressive illness is different from schizophrenia has stood the test of time, although today the concept of manic-depressive illness has been replaced by the broader grouping of mood disorders (also called *affective disorders*). Kraepelin recommended clinical diagnosis on the basis of cross-sectional features and commented that differential diagnosis was most difficult when there was a "mingling of morbid symptoms of both psychoses." Precise boundaries between mood disorders and schizophrenia are still uncertain. The availability of a third category, schizoaffective disorder, has not resolved the difficulties.

Table 4-3: General Medical Conditions That May Cause Secondary (Symptomatic) Psychosis

	Strength of Evidence for a Causal Relationship
Nutritional Deficiency Syndromes	
Pellegra (Vitamin B$_3$, nicotinamide)	+++
Pernicious anemia (Vitamin B$_{12}$, cyanocobalamin)	+++
Vitamin A (retinol)	+
Vitamin D (perhaps via calcium deficiency)	+
Magnesium	+
Selenium	±
Zinc	+
Endocrine Disorders	
Adrenocortical insufficiency (Addison's disease)	+++
Adrenocortical excess (Cushing's syndrome)	+++
Hyperparathyroidism	+++
Hyperthyroidism	+++
Hypoparathyroidism (postsurgical)	++
Hypopituitarism (Sheehan's syndrome)	+
Hypothyroidism	+++

± Hypothesized
+ Primarily anecdotal evidence
++ Supported by some evidence besides anecdotes
+++ Well established

	Strength of Evidence for a Causal Relationship
Metabolic Diseases	
Adrenoleukodystrophy/ adrenomyeloneuropathy	++
Angiokeratoma corporis diffusum (Fabry's disease)	++
GM_2 gangliosidosis	++
Hartnup disease	+++
Hepatolenticular degeneration (Wilson's disease)	+++
Homocystinuria from MTHFR deficiency	+++
Metachromatic leukodystrophy (adult type)	+
Porphyrias	+++
Infectious Diseases	
Cerebral cysts and abscesses	+++
Cerebral malaria	++
Encephalitis caused by herpes simplex	+++
Encephalitis due to other causes	+
HIV encephalopathy	+
Human prion diseases	±
Lyme disease	±
Neurosyphilis (general paresis)	+++
Rheumatic endocarditis	+

continued on next page

Table 4-3: General Medical Conditions That May Cause Secondary (Symptomatic) Psychosis *(continued)*

	Strength of Evidence for a Causal Relationship
Autoimmune Diseases	
Adrenocortical insufficiency (Addison's disease)	+++
Multiple sclerosis	++
Rheumatic fever/chorea	+++
Scleroderma	+
Systemic lupus erythematosus	++
Chromosomal Abnormalities	
Fragile X syndrome (females)	+
Miscellaneous autosomal anomalies	+
Noonan syndrome	+
Velo-cardio-facial syndrome (microdeletion 22q11)	++
XO karyotype (Turner syndrome)	+
XXX karyotype	+
XXY karyotype (Klinefelter syndrome)	++
XYY karyotype	+

±   Hypothesized
+   Primarily anecdotal evidence
++   Supported by some evidence besides anecdotes
+++   Well established

	Strength of Evidence for a Causal Relationship
Other CNS Diseases	
Cerebrovascular lesions	++
Cranial trauma	++
Dementias (especially Pick's disease)	+
Dentatorubral-pallidoluysian atrophy	+
Epilepsies	+++
Familial basal ganglia calcification	+
Friedreich's ataxia	+
Huntington's disease	++
Hydrocephalus of late onset	+++
Immotile cilia syndrome (Kartagener's syndrome)	±
Intracranial tumors	±
Marchiafava-Bignami disease	+
Oculocutaneous albinism	+
Sarcoidosis	+
Schilder's cerebral sclerosis	++
Tuberous sclerosis	++
Uremia	+

Based on Coleman M, Gillberg C: *The Schizophrenias: A Biological Approach to the Schizophrenia Spectrum Disorders.* New York, Springer, 1996.

Table 4-4: Substances That May Cause Psychosis Without Delirium

Drugs of Abuse: During Intoxication
- Alcohol
- Amphetamine, methamphetamine, methylphenidate, and other sympathomimetics
- Cannabis (marijuana, bhang, hashish, sensimilla, tetrahydrocannabinol)
- Cocaine
- Hallucinogens (including ergot compounds, phenylalkamines, indole alkaloids, and 3, 4-methylenedioxymethamphetamine [MDMA or "Ecstasy"])
- Volatile inhalants (eg, gasoline, glue, paint thinners, and halogenated hydrocarbons)
- Opioids
- Phencyclidine and similar-acting compounds (eg, ketamine, cyclohexamine)
- Sedatives, hypnotics, and anxiolytics (including barbiturates, benzodiazepines, carbamates, and similar drugs, but not buspirone)

Drugs of Abuse: During Withdrawal
- Alcohol
- Sedatives, hypnotics, and anxiolytics

Before DSM-III (1980), psychiatrists in the United States diagnosed schizophrenia extremely broadly and mood disorders more narrowly. Cross-national studies verified that many cases diagnosed as schizophrenia in the United States would have been diagnosed as manic-depressive illness in other countries. Today, some discrepancies may occur in the opposite direction, because the DSM-IV concept of

Therapeutic Drug Categories
- Antibiotics (cephalosporins, procaine penicillin)
- Anticholinergic agents (eg, atropine, benztropine, trihexyphenidyl)
- Anticonvulsants (eg, phenytoin, ethosuximide, phenacemide)
- Antidepressants
- Antihypertensive agents (methyldopa, hydralazine)
- Antimalarial agents (chloroquine, quinacrine)
- Antituberculosis agents (isoniazid, cycloserine, iproniazid)
- Antiviral agents (acyclovir, interferon, podophyllin, vidarabine, zidovudine)
- Appetite suppressants (eg, diethylpropion, phentermine, phenylproponolamine)
- Benzodiazepines and benzodiazepine-like hypnotics
- Cardioactive drugs (digitalis, disopyramide, lidocaine, procainamide, apridine)
- Dopaminergic agents (eg, amantadine, levodopa, bromocriptine)

continued on next page

schizophrenia is narrower, and that of mood disorders is broader, than the corresponding categories in ICD-10.

DSM-IV defines mood disorders as those "that have a disturbance in mood as the predominant feature." The most common disturbance in mood is depression, often accompanied by some degree of anxiety. Serious depression is called *major depression*, and some clinicians describe par-

Table 4-4: Substances That May Cause Psychosis Without Delirium *(continued)*

Therapeutic Drug Categories *(continued)*
- Endocrine agents (clomiphene, corticosteroids, thyroid hormones)
- Nonsteroidal anti-inflammatory agents (eg, sulindac, indomethacin, ibuprofen)
- Psychostimulants and sympathomimetics
- Pulmonary agents (albuterol, phenylephrine, ephedrine, pseudoephedrine)
- Miscellaneous (asparaginase, baclofen, cimetidine, cyclosporine, disulfiram, methysurgide, pentazocine)

Toxins
- Arsenic
- Bismuth
- Bromine
- Carbon monoxide
- Copper
- Magnesium
- Manganese
- Mercury
- Thallium

Data from DSM-IV-TR, pp. 191-295. Cummings JL: Organic psychoses: delusional disorders and secondary mania. *Psychiatr Clin North Am* 1986;9:293-312. Coleman M, Gillberg C: *The Schizophrenias: A Biological Approach to the Schizophrenia Spectrum Disorders.* New York, Springer, 1996.

Table 4-5: Syndromal Characteristics of Major Depressive Episodes*

Five or more of the following are required, including one or both of the first two, most of the time on nearly every day for a minimum period of 2 weeks:

- Depressed mood—that is, subjective feelings of sadness or emptiness, or tearfulness observed by others (in children and adolescents, mood may be irritable)
- Markedly diminished interest or pleasure in most activities
- Increase or decrease in appetite or weight
- Insomnia or hypersomnia
- Observable psychomotor agitation or retardation
- Fatigue or loss of energy
- Feelings of worthlessness or of excessive or inappropriate guilt
- Diminished ability to think or concentrate or increased indecisiveness
- Frequent thoughts of death or suicidal ideation or a specific suicidal plan or attempt

*See DSM-IV-TR, p. 356.

tial or less serious depressive syndromes as *minor depression. Mania*, much less common than depression, involves a distinct period in which the mood is persistently elevated, euphoric, expansive, or markedly irritable. *Hypomania* is similar to mania but less severe. In a mixed episode, also called *dysphoric mania*, prominent symptoms of depression and mania occur simultaneously.

Mood disorders are subdivided into *unipolar (depressive) disorders*, which involve episodes of depression but never show features of mania or hypomania, and *bipolar disorders*, in which at least one episode of mania, hypo-

Table 4-6: Syndromal Characteristics of Manic Episodes*

A distinct period of abnormally and persistently elevated or expansive mood, or of marked irritability, lasting at least 1 week (or any duration if hospitalization is required), along with at least three of the following if mood is elevated or expansive or four if mood is primarily irritable:

- Inflated self-esteem or grandiosity
- Substantially decreased need for sleep
- More talkative than usual or pressured speech
- Flight of ideas or racing thoughts
- Marked distractibility (attention is easily sidetracked by irrelevant or unimportant stimuli)
- Increased goal-directed activity, whether successful and productive or not
- Excess in pleasurable activities that have high potential for adverse consequences (eg, spending sprees, sexual indiscretions, foolish investments, reckless driving, risk taking)

*See DSM-IV-TR, p. 362.

mania, or mixed mania and depression has occurred. Depressive episodes also occur in bipolar disorders. The existence of unipolar mania as a distinct disorder is not recognized in DSM-IV or in ICD-10.

Episodes of major depression and mania are recognized by their essential syndromal characteristics, which are outlined in Tables 4-5 and 4-6. Most major depressive episodes and many manic episodes do not include psychotic features and are easily differentiated from schizophrenia.

When mood episodes overlap with symptoms that characterize the active phase of schizophrenia (Table 3-1, Criterion A), differential diagnosis depends on the time course of the latter in relation to the mood syndrome. Determining this time course with confidence may be a difficult clinical task. Three possibilities are depicted graphically in Figures 4-1, 4-2, and 4-3.

Psychotic Features Superimposed on Mood Disorder

If psychotic symptoms have been present only during major depressive or manic episodes (Figure 4-1), the condition is described as psychotic mood disorder or mood disorder with psychotic features. Follow-up studies examining criteria such as demographic characteristics, treatment response, family history, and long-term course of illness strongly support the conclusion that this is a severe mood disorder. It is not schizophrenia, schizoaffective disorder, or something else.

Mood Disorder Superimposed on the Active Phase of Schizophrenia

When a major depressive or manic episode is superimposed on (ie, occurs entirely within) the active phase of schizophrenia, the differential diagnosis requires clinical judgment of whether the mood symptoms are brief in total duration relative to the duration of the active and residual phases of schizophrenia. If the mood syndrome is considered relatively brief (guidelines for making this judgment are not offered), DSM-IV recommends a diagnosis of depressive disorder not otherwise specified (NOS) or bipolar disorder NOS in addition to schizophrenia. This situation (Figure 4-2) may be a true concurrence of schizophrenia and mood disorder.

Schizoaffective Disorder

During schizoaffective disorder, an episode of mood disorder overlaps incompletely or extensively with symptoms of the active phase of schizophrenia (Figure 4-3). In either case, there must be at least one uninterrupted epi-

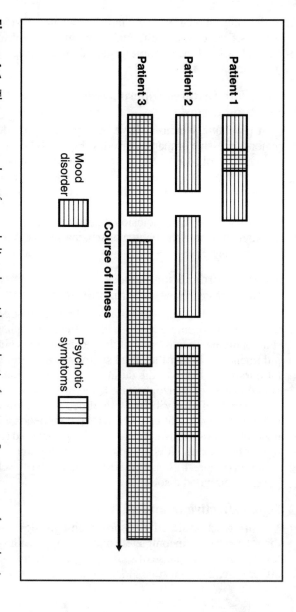

Figure 4-1: Three examples of mood disorder with psychotic features. Symptoms of psychosis (delusions, hallucinations) are present only during periods of mood disorder.

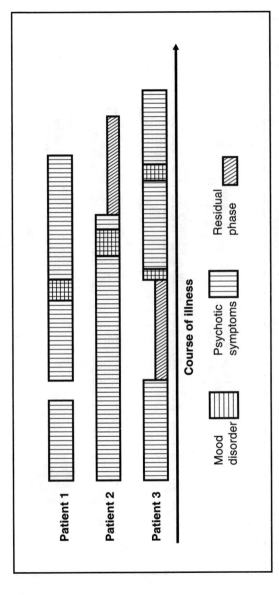

Figure 4-2: Three examples of mood disorder superimposed on psychosis. Mood episodes are entirely contained within the active phase of schizophrenia, and the total duration of mood symptoms is brief relative to the duration of active- and residual-phase symptoms.

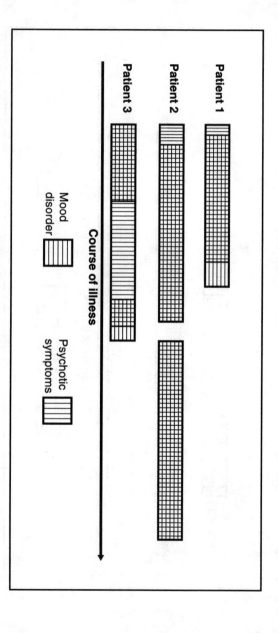

Figure 4-3: Three examples of schizoaffective disorder. Mood symptoms and psychotic symptoms overlap substantially, and at least one episode also contains 2 weeks of psychotic symptoms without mood symptoms.

sode of illness that includes a period in which mood and psychotic symptoms overlap and at least 2 weeks in which psychotic symptoms are present without any prominent mood symptoms.

Schizoaffective was first used to describe illnesses characterized by sudden onset, marked emotional turmoil, distortion of the outside world, and recovery within a few months. Subsequently, the meaning has shifted to describe conditions in which typical schizophrenia symptoms are intermixed with symptoms typical of mood disorder.

In DSM-II, schizoaffective was a subtype of schizophrenia. In DSM-III, schizoaffective disorder was listed in a chapter titled "Psychotic Disorders Not Elsewhere Classified," separate from schizophrenia and affective disorders. It was the only diagnosis in that manual for which no criteria were proposed, attesting to its clinical importance and the lack of consensus on its definition. It was included "for those instances in which the clinician is unable to make a differential diagnosis with any degree of certainty between affective disorder and either schizophreniform disorder or schizophrenia." This meaning coincides with the recommendation of Blacker and Tsuang that schizoaffective be used to describe "patients whose psychotic symptoms are not clearly linked to their affective episodes."

In DSM-IV, schizoaffective disorder is grouped with all other psychotic disorders in a single chapter. As described previously, diagnosis is based on the time course of psychotic symptoms relative to mood episodes. The criteria make no reference to the content of the psychotic symptoms, such as their congruence or incongruence with the mood symptoms. Some psychiatrists, nevertheless, record this diagnosis for patients whose psychotic symptoms are strikingly incongruent with their mood symptoms, regardless of the temporal pattern of the overlap. This conforms with the definition of schizoaffective disorder in ICD-10 as a mixture of a mood syndrome with psychotic symptoms considered typical of schizophrenia and not consistent with mood. It seems probable that the boundaries of this category will remain controversial.

Tsuang, Levitt, and Simpson reviewed published studies of schizoaffective disorder and concluded that this is most likely a heterogeneous grouping containing some patients who have 'good prognosis' schizophrenia, some who have severe mood disorders, and perhaps some who have a residual condition that is neither schizophrenia nor mood disorder. Relatives of patients with the schizoaffective diagnosis have elevated risk for both schizophrenia and mood disorders. Suicide rates for schizoaffective disorder are similar to those for severe mood disorder, somewhat higher than for schizophrenia. Optimal treatment usually requires cotherapy with antipsychotic medication and mood stabilizing or antidepressant medication.

Postschizophrenic Depression

Many patients experience an episode of major depression following an illness that seems to be typical schizophrenia. ICD-10 recognizes this occurrence as a subtype or phase of schizophrenia, which it calls *postschizophrenic depression*. DSM-IV includes postpsychotic depressive disorder of schizophrenia in Appendix B, Criteria Sets and Axes Provided for Further Study, and defines it as a major depressive episode contained entirely within the residual phase of schizophrenia.

Psychotic Disorders
Considered Different from Schizophrenia

DSM-IV lists nine conditions under the heading "Schizophrenia and Other Psychotic Disorders." Three of these diagnoses, schizoaffective disorder, substance-induced psychotic disorder, and psychotic disorder caused by general medical condition, were examined previously. The remaining five forms of nonschizophrenic psychotic disorder are described in Table 4-7.

Table 4-7: Other Primary Psychotic Disorders Listed in DSM-IV

Note: The following diagnoses are excluded if the person has ever met criteria for schizophrenia or schizoaffective disorder, currently meets criteria for mood disorder with psychotic features, or has a general medical condition, is using substances, or is going through substance withdrawal judged to be a direct physiologic cause of the psychotic symptoms.

• *Brief psychotic disorder:* Significant psychotic symptoms are present for at least 1 day but resolve within 1 month, with a full return to the previous level of functioning.

• *Schizophreniform disorder:* Criterion A for schizophrenia (Table 3-1) is met for at least 1 month, but the person has never had a continuous period of illness (prodromal, active, and residual phases) lasting as long as 6 months.

• *Delusional disorder:* The person has nonbizarre delusions, not accompanied by any other symptoms from Criterion A for schizophrenia, for at least 1 month.

• *Shared psychotic disorder (folie à deux):* A person accepts a delusional belief in the context of a close personal relationship with another person who has the same delusion.

• *Psychotic disorder not otherwise specified:* A residual category for a psychotic disorder not meeting criteria for any condition mentioned above.

Schizophreniform and Brief Psychotic Disorders

These conditions are thought to be different from schizophrenia because of their short duration and lack of deterioration. These diagnoses are not appropriate if the patient has previously met criteria for schizophrenia or schizoaffective disorder or now meets criteria for a psychotic mood disorder.

In brief psychotic disorder, some combination of delusions, hallucinations, grossly disorganized speech, and grossly disorganized or catatonic behavior are present for at least 1 day but completely resolve within 1 month. It has long been known that single psychotic episodes of brief duration tend to be followed by full recovery without future psychosis or deterioration.

In two-thirds of cases, schizophreniform disorder probably represents a mild form or the early stage of schizophrenia. This diagnosis is used when the person has had at least one episode of Criterion A symptoms (Table 3-1) within a continuous period of illness lasting longer than 1 month but less than 6 months. It is often recorded provisionally during treatment of a first episode and then changed to schizophrenia if symptoms are still present after 6 months.

To identify those patients with schizophreniform disorder who are less likely to eventually have schizophrenia, DSM-IV suggests the specification "with good prognostic features" when two or more of the following are found: (1) rapid onset of prominent psychotic symptoms (within 4 weeks of the first noticeable change in functioning); (2) confusion or perplexity at the height of the psychotic episode; (3) good social and occupational functioning before the onset of psychosis; and (4) absence of flat or blunted affect. These are among the strongest predictors from Table 3-9 for 'good prognosis schizophrenia.'

Psychotic Disorders Restricted to Delusions

When Kraepelin proposed the fundamental distinction between dementia praecox (schizophrenia) and manic-depressive illness, he also described a third category of psychotic illness, which he called *paranoia*. In modern vernacular usage, this term has acquired a connotation suggesting an attitude of suspiciousness, mistrust, and irritability that is not necessarily psychotic and may not even be psychopathologic.

Kraepelin, by contrast, was referring to a disorder characterized by delusions that are logically structured, internally consistent, and restricted to a single theme, which need not be persecutory. The delusions are not secondary to an abnormality of mood and are not caused by the direct physiologic effects of a general medical condition or substance.

Kraepelin believed this was different from schizophrenia because the personality remained relatively intact, affective capacity was preserved, functioning did not markedly deteriorate, and the person's logical abilities were not affected except in matters related to the delusion. In other words, the delusions are *encapsulated* within an otherwise normal personality.

In DSM-IV and ICD-10, this condition is named *delusional disorder*. The DSM-IV criteria require that the delusions persist longer than 1 month and that the content be 'nonbizarre,' that is, it must involve a theme that is experienced in real life, such as being followed, poisoned, infected, loved by someone else, betrayed by a spouse or lover, or afflicted by a disease. Auditory hallucinations, grossly disorganized or incoherent speech, grossly disorganized or catatonic behavior, and negative symptoms must not be present. If episodes of depression or mania occur concurrently with the delusions, the mood symptoms are relatively brief in total duration relative to the delusions.

Hallucinations in tactile and olfactory modalities are permitted, provided they are consistent with the delusional theme. For example, in delusional parasitosis (belief that one has a parasitic infestation), the patient may have tactile experiences consistent with the belief.

Subtypes of delusional disorder are defined according to the delusional themes. Subtypes listed in DSM-IV are erotomanic type, grandiose type, jealous type, persecutory type, somatic type, and mixed type.

Long-term follow-ups of delusional disorder find that a proportion of patients eventually show substantial deterioration, negative symptoms, or auditory hallucinations, suggesting that the condition was a form of schizophrenia or schizoaffective disorder all along. Some cases, however, persist in stable form indefinitely, and therefore seem to be different from schizophrenia.

Many patients with delusional disorder maintain a high level of social and occupational functioning. Often, their emotions and behavior seem entirely normal when the delusional ideation is not being examined or acted on. Other patients may show deterioration in functioning as a direct consequence of the delusions. For example, they may become reclusive and secretive to escape the threats suggested by the delusional content. Even in these patients, the quality of impairment and deterioration is different from schizophrenia.

Another DSM-IV diagnosis in which symptoms are restricted to delusions (nonbizarreness is not required) is called *shared psychotic disorder*. In clinical literature, it is often called *folie à deux*. In this disorder, a patient comes to accept as truth the delusional beliefs of another person in the context of a close relationship and, usually, social isolation. This person may be emotionally needy or psychiatrically vulnerable but often is not truly psychotic. Munro summarizes this irony by saying that "the belief is psychotic but the believer is not."

Psychotic Disorder Not Otherwise Specified

This is a residual category for psychotic disorders not meeting criteria for any of the specific conditions explained previously. Examples would include non-Schneiderian auditory hallucinations without any other abnormality and bizarre delusions without any other symptoms or functional deterioration.

Another example is the condition Kraepelin described as *paraphrenia*, in which the person has mixed delusions and auditory hallucinations. Unlike schizophrenia, affect is preserved and appropriate, and there is no intellectual deterioration, visual hallucination, incoherence, marked loosening of associations, or grossly disorganized behavior. Munro and others argue that this should be included as a distinct category in the DSM and ICD.

Suggested Readings

Coleman M, Gillberg C: *The Schizophrenias: A Biological Approach to the Schizophrenia Spectrum Disorders.* New York, Springer, 1996.

Cummings JL: Organic psychoses: delusional disorders and secondary mania. *Psychiatr Clin North Am* 1986;9:293-311.

Kane JM, Selzer J: Considerations on 'organic' exclusion criteria for schizophrenia. *Schizophr Bull* 1991;17:69-73.

Kendler KH: The nosologic validity of mood-incongruent psychotic affective illness. In Widiger T, Frances AJ, Pincus HA, eds. *DSM-IV Sourcebook, Volume I.* Washington, DC, American Psychiatric Association, 1994.

Levitt JJ, Tsuang MT: The heterogeneity of schizoaffective disorder: implications for treatment. *Am J Psychiatry* 1988;145:926-936.

Lishman MA: *Organic Psychiatry: The Psychological Consequences of Cerebral Disorder,* 3rd ed. Oxford, Blackwell Science Ltd, 1998.

Munro A: *Delusional Disorder: Paranoia and Related Illnesses.* Cambridge, Cambridge University Press, 1999.

Nasrallah HA: The neuropsychiatry of schizophrenia and related disorders. In: Yudofsky SC, Hales RE, eds. *The American Psychiatric Press Textbook of Neuropsychiatry,* 2nd ed. Washington, DC, American Psychiatric Press, 1992.

Popkin MK, Tucker GJ: Mental disorders due to a general medical condition and substance-induced disorders: mood, anxiety, psychotic, catatonic, and personality disorders. In Widiger T, Frances AJ, Pincus HA, eds. *DSM-IV Sourcebook, Volume I.* Washington, DC, American Psychiatric Association, 1994.

Tsuang MT, Levitt JJ, Simpson JC: Schizoaffective disorder. In Hirsch SR, Weinberger DA, eds. *Schizophrenia.* Oxford, Blackwell Science Ltd, 1995.

Chapter 5

Schizophrenia Through the Life Span

The Course and Outcome of Schizophrenia

The modern concept of schizophrenia originated in Emil Kraepelin's hypothesis that dementia praecox was a homogeneous category of psychotic illness. In its name and definition, he identified two characteristics as its essential features: onset in adolescence or young adulthood and a deteriorating course tending toward mental decrepitude. The distinctive longitudinal pattern was Kraepelin's gold standard for the diagnosis until a specific neuropathology could be identified. The gold standard, however, was not available to the working clinician, so Kraepelin suggested cross-sectional diagnostic criteria that he believed were predictors of course and outcome.

Eugen Bleuler disputed Kraepelin's claims of homogeneity, the necessity of onset in young adulthood, and the inevitability of deterioration. He renamed the condition *the group of schizophrenias*, argued that course and outcome were variable rather than distinctive, and proposed a group of fundamental symptoms as the gold standard for diagnosis.

A century of research and clinical experience supports Bleuler's contention that course and outcome are variable. Differences in diagnostic criteria explain only a portion of the heterogeneity. Even Kraepelin reported that 15% of his patients eventually achieved lasting remission and revised his emphasis on deterioration. Regardless of how schizophrenia is diagnosed, its course and outcome are more variable and less predictable than those of any other disease of comparable severity.

Today, a rigid Kraepelinian might still argue that any illness with a good outcome is not schizophrenia. Since no combination of clinical features has been found to predict outcome with a high degree of accuracy, this position has not led to scientific progress.

Modern diagnostic criteria differ in requiring chronicity as a defining characteristic. The *International Classification of Diseases*, Revision 10 (ICD-10) and the fourth edition of the *Diagnostic and Statistical Manual of Mental Disorders* (DSM-IV) agree that short illnesses should not be diagnosed as schizophrenia. ICD-10 requires 1 month of psychotic illness, while DSM-IV requires a 6-month period of illness that includes a psychotic phase but may also include nonpsychotic prodromal and residual symptoms.

Methodologic differences in outcome studies contribute to discrepancies but cannot explain the universal finding of heterogeneity. Factors such as initial cohort characteristics, the criteria by which schizophrenia was diagnosed, the duration and success of follow-up procedures, and definitions and criteria for outcome categories do have some effect on reported statistics. Westermeyer and Harrow conclude that perfect studies do not exist, and that "Knowledge regarding course and outcome for schizophrenia is necessarily a composite of many different researches studying different samples and using different measures."

Patterns of Clinical Course

Clinical course refers to the longitudinal pattern of an illness over an extended time, usually beginning at onset and ending at its definitive conclusion or at the end of life. Although a multitude of different course patterns have been described for schizophrenia, we will focus on three dichotomies.

The *epoch of onset*, which refers to the initial manifestations of the illness up to and including the beginning of psychosis, may be insidious (gradual) or acute (rapid). Some authors report nearly equal proportions of the two types, while others report a preponderance of insidious onsets, particularly in the United States.

The *middle epoch* may be continuous or undulating (episodic); the latter implies symptomatic periods with identifiable beginning and ending points, although residual symptoms may be present between episodes. These two patterns are approximately equal in frequency.

The *late epoch (outcome)* may be classified as improved or even asymptomatic versus not improved or deteriorating. Regardless of diagnostic criteria and initial sample characteristics, all studies have found significant numbers of patients with good outcomes. Moreover, the proportion of good outcomes seems to have increased during the past 50 years. It is unclear whether this trend is attributable to changes in treatment, changes in public policy, changes in the severity of the illness itself, or some combination of these factors.

Of great interest is the seemingly paradoxical finding that good outcomes are more frequent in less developed countries than in highly industrialized nations such as the United States. The best explanatory hypothesis is that social or environmental advantages, or a lower degree of social pressures and pathogenic environmental conditions, outweigh the benefits of superior treatments in determining outcome.

When patient cohorts are sufficiently large and representative, all eight possible combinations of these dichotomies are observed, but in differing frequencies. The least common pattern is acute onset, continuous course, and no improvement. Also relatively uncommon are cases with acute onset, continuous course, and good outcome and those with insidious onset, continuous course, and good or poor outcome. The most frequent patterns in the United States have insidious onset and undulating course.

Several authors have found that subsequent disease trajectory may be influenced by the duration of untreated psychotic symptoms at illness onset. When antipsychotic drug treatment of the first psychotic episode is significantly delayed, the patient is more likely to have a multiepisode course of illness, will spend more days in the hospital during the rest of his or her life, and is less likely to have an outcome described as complete recovery.

Outcome Studies

This type of study focuses on a patient's status at a single point in time following the index episode of illness, usually without obtaining data to determine how that status came about.

Johnstone reviewed studies published between 1932 and 1980 in which the mean follow-up period was at least 10 years and the reported outcomes could be graded as recovered, improved, or not improved. Across these 22 studies totaling more than 4,000 patients, the proportion classified as recovered ranged from 2% to 52% (median 26%); the proportion reported as improved ranged from 8% to 46% (median again 26%); and the proportion not improved ranged from 17% to 80% (median 50%). Among seven studies published since 1970, the proportion of cases not improved ranged from 17% to 47% (median 35%), confirming the trend toward better outcomes in recent years.

Outcome Characteristics

For any mental disorder, long-term outcome is a multidimensional variable. Because schizophrenia is a pervasive and disabling condition, however, many studies have focused on relatively simple indices such as complete recovery, need for rehospitalization, levels of positive and negative symptoms, quality of interpersonal relationships, ability to work, and mortality.

Several studies have looked for full recovery, including total and lasting remission of all symptoms, no need for medication, resumption of the highest prepsychotic level of functioning, and being viewed as not mentally ill by self, family, and others. Applying slight variations of this straightforward definition, six investigators have reported rates of full recovery between 19% and 30%.

Rehospitalization rates are high for persons with schizophrenia. Summarizing available studies, Westermeyer and Harrow concluded that 40% to 50% of patients will be rehospitalized during the first year following discharge, and up to 85% will eventually be rehospitalized at some time.

The likelihood of rehospitalization depends on other variables besides the course of illness. There are many psychotic patients living outside of hospitals, with varying degrees of success, depending on hospital admission policies and availability and effectiveness of community resources. Almost all patients who are not psychotic remain unhospitalized, even when residual impairment is substantial.

Two factors that have been shown to strongly increase rehospitalization rates are not taking maintenance medication and exposure to an emotionally toxic environment. During the first year after hospitalization, patients who continue to take antipsychotic medication have a risk of rehospitalization of 1.5% to 3% per month. For those taking placebo or no medication, the risk is 8% to 15% per month. These data are from studies of traditional neuroleptics (old antipsychotics) and may not be applicable to patients treated with the newer agents.

The operationally defined concept of emotional toxicity is called *expressed emotion (EE)* and refers to the attitudes of persons with whom the patient is in frequent contact. High EE includes frequent expressions of hostility, disapproval, or dissatisfaction toward the patient, or emotional overinvolvement in the patient's daily life. The detrimental effects of high EE are seen in other forms of severe mental disorder besides schizophrenia. Research has shown that they can be reduced by psychoeducational interventions directed toward members of the patient's family or by minimizing the amount of time the patient is in contact with sources of high EE. Maintenance medication also decreases but does not entirely eliminate the impact of a high EE environment.

Most patients continue to experience psychiatric symptoms after discharge from the hospital. At any time after hospital discharge, 60% to 75% of patients show attenuated or full-blown positive symptoms (eg, hallucinations, delusions, bizarre thoughts and experiences), about 50% show some type of thought disorder, and 30% to 60% show prominent negative symptoms or cognitive impairment. As patients age, negative symptoms tend to increase, and positive symptoms tend to decrease. High levels of anxiety and depressive symptoms are also found at all stages of follow-up, but these do not differentiate patients with schizophrenia from those with other severe mental disorders.

Although the quality of interpersonal relationships following an episode of schizophrenia is difficult to define and measure, self-reports and some quantitative assessments have been studied. Many patients with schizophrenia self-report poor social relationships. On average, patients are markedly below control subjects in frequency of marriage, success as a parent, size of social networks, frequency of social contacts, and number of confiding relationships.

For most patients, an episode of schizophrenia is followed by a serious and long-lasting reduction in capacity for occupational functioning. Follow-up studies have reported full-time employment rates ranging from 15% to 56%, but the higher percentages come from studies that defined schizophrenia more broadly. Patients with significant residual symptoms have been found to have unemployment rates as high as 85%.

Persons with schizophrenia have increased mortality rates compared with the general population but not in comparison with persons who have other severe mental illnesses. Much of the increase is explained by the suicide rate, which is reported as 10% to 15%. Over a lifetime, this suicide rate is exceeded only by patients with severe mood disorder. Some authors report that suicide risk is greatest in young male patients in early stages of the illness, and they state that the risk of suicide is greater for schizophrenia than for any other condition during the first 5 years.

Other significant causes of increased mortality include all forms of unnatural death (homicide, accident, environmental causes), cardiovascular illness, and pulmonary infections.

Conclusions

P. J. McKenna remarked that, so far as course and outcome are concerned, "schizophrenia follows no rules but its own." Most modern authors, however, would agree with the following summary statements: (1) However schizophrenia is defined, there is considerable heterogeneity of outcomes, ranging from excellent adjustment to total disability. (2) For about 75% of patients, schizophrenia is a chronic disease that causes some degree of disability for the rest of their life. (3) The average outcome of schizophrenia is worse than that of other major mental illnesses, including severe mood disorders. (4) The course of an individual schizophrenic illness is extremely difficult to predict; unexpected turns for the better or worse may occur at any stage. (5) For most patients, the disease process does not progress indefinitely. At some point, usually within 5 to 10 years of onset, deterioration reaches a plateau, which will remain relatively stable over a long time or be followed by signs of improvement.

Developmental Precursors of Schizophrenia

Although onset of frank schizophrenia most commonly occurs in adolescence or young adulthood, the importance of genetic predisposition and the increased risk associated with early life events (eg, perinatal hypoxia) suggest that the disease trajectory may begin long before its clinical appearance.

A modest body of evidence supports the hypothesis that children who receive a diagnosis of schizophrenia later in life show subtle abnormalities of development and early functioning that may reflect brain dysfunction already present. Following is a review of findings from three types of studies: (1) 'fossil evidence' in adult patients with schizophrenia, which documents a developmental aberration that occurred many years previously; (2) birth cohort studies that systematically assess children throughout development, providing data that can be analyzed in 'followback' studies after adult disease is identified; and (3) prospective studies of infants at ultrahigh risk for later development of schizophrenia.

Fossil Studies

Adult patients with schizophrenia show increased rates of dermatoglyphic abnormalities and minor physical anomalies.

The formation and positioning of palmar dermal ridges occurs during the second trimester of fetal development, coinciding closely with a massive migration of neurons from the periventricular proliferative zone to the cerebral cortex. Dermal cell migration is known to be vulnerable to environmental insults, but ridge patterns are permanent once formed and cannot be altered by postnatal events. Abnormalities in ridge count or shape and the degree of left-right asymmetry are indices of a developmental disruption that can be timed precisely.

Configural abnormalities and excessive asymmetry are observed more frequently in persons with schizophrenia than in control groups, including persons with other serious mental disorders. Monozygotic twin pairs who are discordant for schizophrenia show greater dermatoglyphic differences than concordant twin pairs, with more abnormality in the affected co-twin. This has been interpreted as evidence for a difference in intrauterine environment during the second trimester, which presumably affected brain development and dermatoglyphic patterns in the co-twin with schizophrenia.

Minor physical anomalies, which by definition have no significance for health or appearance, are found most frequently in the face, ears, hands, and feet. Individual anomalies are markers of developmental disturbances that can be accurately timed in the trajectory of normal fetal development. Several studies have found increased rates of specific anomalies associated with schizophrenia, and those using a comprehensive scale reported higher total anomaly scores for schizophrenia. Particularly prominent were abnormalities involving the mouth and palate, which develop simultaneously with the brain from a common embryonic ectoderm. Higher anomaly scores are associated with more dermatoglyphic abnormalities, poorer premorbid functioning, and earlier onset of psychosis, especially in males. Increased rates of anomalies are also found in persons with other psychotic disorders.

Birth Cohort Followback Studies

These studies begin with a cohort of all persons born within a specific period and region and look for associations of adult schizophrenia with other available data. This methodology has linked increased risk for schizophrenia with maternal starvation during the first trimester, prenatal or perinatal brain damage resulting from pregnancy and birth complications, maternal exposure to influenza (not necessarily clinical infection) during the second trimester, delayed developmental milestones during the first 2 years (especially sitting, standing, walking, and speaking), greater frequency of speech abnormalities between ages 2 and 15 years, lower cognitive/academic achievement on standardized tests at ages 8, 11, and 15 years, and preference for solitary play at ages 4 and 6 years.

High-Risk Studies

These studies follow infants born to parents who have schizophrenia, from birth through the entire period of risk for schizophrenia. Although requiring effort and resources over a long period, they have the advantage of starting with a population that has a 10-fold greater risk for schizophrenia than an unselected birth cohort. Several such studies are now in progress, and preliminary results have been reported.

Between 25% and 50% of high-risk children show a combination of obvious and subtle developmental abnormalities during infancy and childhood. Reported findings include hypotonia and poor cuddling behavior; delayed developmental milestones; an increased frequency of soft (nonlocalizing) neurologic signs, particularly involving motor coordination; and deficits in attention and information processing.

In one of the earlier studies, Fish described a *pandysmaturational syndrome* consisting of abnormalities of physical growth, gross motor skills, visual-motor coordination, cognitive development, proprioceptive and vestibular responses, and muscle tone. Although the features tended to wane and often disappear later in childhood, Fish hypothesized that this syndrome of neurointegrative deficits was evidence of a major disorganization of central nervous system development. She subsequently reported that all seven of her subjects who met diagnostic criteria for schizophrenia or schizotypal personality disorder by age 22 years had shown this syndrome in infancy. Other investigators are reporting similar findings, but these reports must be considered provisional because most subjects have not yet finished the period of risk for schizophrenia.

Walker et al studied persons with schizophrenia whose parents had recorded their infant and childhood development on home movies. In a blind evaluation of the movies by trained raters, they found that toddlers who went on to have schizophrenia could be clearly distinguished from their nonaffected siblings by a greater frequency of negative affects, poorer motor skills, and higher rate of neuromotor abnormalities, particularly on the left side of the body. The observed differences were much less evident after 2 years of age.

Summary

Studies of neurodevelopmental precursors of schizophrenia look for evidence of abnormal brain functioning early in the lives of persons who develop schizophrenia many years later. Many positive findings have been reported, but each is modest in magnitude and seems to affect only a minority of patients. Most abnormalities are not unique to schizophrenia but are also found in association with other psychotic disorders and severe mood disorders. Some findings have not been confirmed or replicated in independent studies. Persons who show one type of abnormality often do not show other types. Many of the nonfossilized abnormalities disappear before the onset of schizophrenia and probably represent developmental delays rather than failures. Nevertheless, this body of evidence supports the hypothesis that a disease trajectory leading to adult schizophrenia can be detected early in the lives of some patients. A more optimistic interpretation is that signs of high vulnerability to schizophrenia can be found early in life and may lead to preventive interventions.

Prepubertal Schizophrenia

Although in most cases of schizophrenia the onset of psychosis is in late adolescence or young adulthood, instances of prepubertal onset have been reported since early in the 20th century. Prepubertal schizophrenia has sometimes been described as *dementia precocissima*.

Diagnosis of psychosis in children has been more problematic than in adults. In DSM-II, only one diagnostic category was available for psychotic children. It was called *schizophrenia, childhood type*, and included children who would today be diagnosed in the autistic spectrum. Kumra, Nicolson, and Rapoport describe the distinction between early-onset psychosis (up to age 3 years) from later childhood psychosis (beginning at age 5 years or older) as "one of the most important diagnostic advances in child psychiatry, separating autism from true childhood schizophrenia." Much research has confirmed that autism and other pervasive developmental disorders are unlike schizophrenia in many important ways.

True prepubertal schizophrenia has an estimated morbid risk rate of 0.02%. This is less than half the prevalence of autistic disorder in the same population and 1/50 of the morbid risk of postpubertal schizophrenia.

Today, the same criteria are used for diagnosis of schizophrenia in all age groups (Table 3-1). The most difficult differential diagnosis to eliminate is childhood bipolar disorder. Children who do not meet full criteria for schizophrenia but have a severe mental disorder with transient psychotic symptoms, severely disruptive behavior, and learning disabilities are sometimes described as having *multidimensional impairment*. Because this condition shares many similarities with schizophrenia in children of the same age, it may be within the schizophrenic spectrum (ie, a partial or milder form of schizophrenia with shared genetic predisposition).

Prepubertal schizophrenia seems to be the same condition as severe adult schizophrenia. Compared with adults who have poor outcomes, child patients have similar abnormalities in premorbid functioning, neuropsychologic testing, autonomic nervous system functioning, smooth pursuit eye tracking, and brain structure. Compared with nonpsychotic children who go on to have schizophrenia as adults, children with schizophrenia have the same kinds of developmental disturbances, generally in higher frequency and more severe degree. Additionally, children with schizophrenia sometimes show transient symptoms similar to those of autism (eg, stereotyped movements, poor social contact, odd use of language).

Late-Onset Schizophrenia

It is important to distinguish the term *late-life schizophrenia*, which refers to schizophrenia in an elderly person (usually older than 65), regardless of age of onset, from *late-onset schizophrenia*, which implies true onset after age 45 years. The latter has sometimes been called *dementia tardiva*. It is relatively rare, presents special diagnostic problems, has been studied little, and raises nosologic questions that are now debated. DSM-III attempted to bypass the nosologic debate by requiring onset younger than age 45 years for the diagnosis of schizophrenia. This criterion did not reduce controversy and was dropped from DSM-IV.

The reported prevalence of schizophrenia in elderly populations ranges between 0.1% and 1.0%. Within this group, most have typical schizophrenia that began before age 40 or 45 years. Only about 1 case in 10 had onset after age 40 years, and nearly all of these cases were women.

Until recently, studies of schizophrenia in the elderly have not distinguished patients in the late stage of typical schizophrenia from those in whom onset was atypically late. This made it impossible to determine whether differences in comparison with younger patients are attributable only to age and chronicity (and perhaps to treatment history) or whether late-onset cases are a distinct subgroup. This is the primary question of interest about late-onset schizophrenia.

Recent investigations have compared patients with late-onset schizophrenia to different age groups of patients with typical schizophrenia. On many measures, such as imaging studies of brain morphology and function, neuropsychologic testing, and treatment response, late-onset schizophrenia is similar to typical schizophrenia at the same stage of chronicity. There is a preponderance of women in late-onset groups, which is consistent with the well-documented finding of a later average age of onset in women with typical schizophrenia. The most interesting and important differences have involved symptom patterns.

When patients with similar duration of illness are compared, late-onset schizophrenia shows similar levels of positive symptoms, significantly lower levels of negative symptoms, and much lower levels of thought disorder than typical schizophrenia. Some differences in the content of positive symptoms have been described. Patients with late-onset schizophrenia usually have persecutory delusions and auditory hallucinations. Schneiderian delusions of passivity, visual hallucinations, catatonic symptoms, and hebephrenic symptoms are much less common than in typical schizophrenia.

When patients at the same age are compared, those with late-onset schizophrenia have higher levels of positive symptoms and much lower levels of negative symptoms than those with typical schizophrenia. These differences increase with age. This is consistent with the trend for positive symptoms to decrease and negative symptoms to increase with age in typical schizophrenia and with the frequent observation that late-onset schizophrenia is a more static condition in which symptoms do not evolve over time.

Some studies also have reported that relatives of patients with late-onset schizophrenia have increased rates of mood disorders but not of schizophrenia. This finding is less robust than the differences in symptom patterns.

It is still unclear whether late-onset schizophrenia is only a mild form of typical schizophrenia, a distinct subtype, or a separate disease group. Some clinicians believe that the condition diverges from typical schizophrenia with increasing age and prefer to use late-onset schizophrenia as a distinct diagnosis. When onset is after age 65, the terms *very late-onset schizophrenia* or *very late-onset schizophrenia-like psychosis* may be used.

Suggested Readings

Carpenter WT, Kirkpatrick B: The heterogeneity of the long-term course of schizophrenia. *Schizophr Bull* 1988;14:645-652.

Green MF, Satz P, Gaier DJ, et al: Minor physical anomalies in schizophrenia. *Schizophr Bull* 1989;15:91-99.

Howard R, Rabins PV, Castle DJ, eds. *Late Onset Schizophrenia*. Philadelphia, Wrightson Biomedical Publishing Ltd, 1999.

Jeste DV, Gilbert PL, et al: Late-life schizophrenia. In Hirsch SR, Weinberger DR, eds. *Schizophrenia*. Oxford, Blackwell Science Ltd, 1995.

Kumra S, Nicolson R, Rapoport JL: Childhood onset schizophrenia: research update. In Zipursky RB, Schulz SC, eds. *The Early Stages of Schizophrenia*. Washington, DC, American Psychiatric Press, 2002.

McGlashan TH: A selective review of recent North American long-term followup studies of schizophrenia. *Schizophr Bull* 1988; 14:515-542.

Miller HJ, von Zerssen D: Course and outcome of schizophrenia. In Hirsch SR, Weinberger DR, eds. *Schizophrenia*. Oxford, Blackwell Science Ltd, 1995.

Rapoport JL, ed. *Childhood Onset of "Adult" Psychopathology*. Washington, DC, American Psychiatric Press, 2000.

Waddington JL, Lane A, Scully PJ, et al: Neurodevelopmental and neuroprogressive processes in schizophrenia: antithetical or complementary, over a lifetime trajectory of disease? *Psychiatr Clin North Am* 1998;21:123-149.

Westermeyer JF, Harrow M: Course and outcome in schizophrenia. In Tsuang MT, Simpson JC, eds. *Handbook of Schizophrenia, Volume 3: Nosology, Epidemiology, and Genetics of Schizophrenia*. New York, Elsevier Science, 1988.

Wilcox JA, Nasrallah HA: Childhood head trauma and psychosis. *Psychiatry Res* 1987;21:303-306.

Chapter 6

Neurobiology of Schizophrenia

This chapter summarizes empirical differences in brain structure or functioning that distinguish patients with schizophrenia from suitable controls. The neuropharmacology of dopamine (DA) and serotonin (5-HT) is reviewed, and its relevance to the treatment of schizophrenia and its possible role in pathophysiology are examined.

This body of scientific literature is huge and growing rapidly. It is also replete with contradictory findings and controversy. Many discrepancies and controversies result from differences in subject selection. For groups with schizophrenia, sources of possible confounding include diagnostic criteria, chronicity, treatment history, and medication. For patients and control subjects, extraneous variables such as age, sex, education, medical history, and substance use may skew the findings.

This examination will not be a critical analysis or comprehensive review. Instead, a coherent picture that is becoming discernible is described, focusing on the results that seem robust and the interpretations that are more widely accepted.

Many reported differences are best understood as a 'distributional shift' in which distributions of measurements from patients and controls are similar in shape but centered around different means (Figure 6-1). The direction of the shift depends on the variable. If the control group

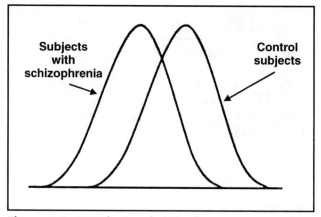

Figure 6-1: Distributional shift of measurements from schizophrenia group relative to control group.

defines what is 'normal,' there will be more patients than controls with abnormal measurements. Considerable overlap remains between the two groups, however, so most patients will be within the 'normal' range. Because the shifted distribution remains unimodal, it can be argued that the abnormality affects the entire population and is not limited to a subgroup of statistical 'outliers.'

Neurology and Neuropsychology
The Clinical Neurologic Examination

The clinical neurologic examination assesses the function and structure of a patient's nervous system without invasive procedures or special equipment. Since schizophrenia involves abnormalities of brain function, a clinical neurologic examination is an important step in evaluating every patient being considered for this diagnosis. Specific findings in the examination may lead to the discovery that a nonpsychiatric condition causes the patient's psychotic symptoms (Table 4-3). Additionally, many patients with schizophrenia also have comorbid conditions (both psychiatric and nonpsychiatric) that require attention when planning treatment.

Most patients with schizophrenia show one or more neurologic 'soft signs.' These are abnormal findings or unusual performance that lack significance for central nervous system (CNS) localization. Table 6-1 lists many soft signs that have been reported in schizophrenia.

Cadet, Rickler, and Weinberger have remarked, "Interpreting the mental status examination in neurological terms is particularly challenging in patients with schizophrenia. Aspects of the exam may suggest diagnosable focal or diffuse disease of the CNS." Such findings, nevertheless, often have primarily psychiatric explanations.

For example, psychiatric and nonpsychiatric conditions may cause catatonic symptoms. Abnormalities of arousal and attention may be caused by negative symptoms (eg, alogia, amotivation), positive symptoms (eg, disturbing psychotic thoughts, hallucinations), or refusal to cooperate. Delusional thinking may cause disorientation. Idiosyncratic answers may be given to tests of calculation and other abilities. Tests of abstract thinking (similarities, proverbs) may produce answers that are bizarre, self-referential, overinclusive, or tangential. Erratic performance in carrying out tasks on command may resemble neurologic dyspraxia.

Communication and speech problems such as dysarthria and dysprosody are frequent in schizophrenia and often precede the onset of psychosis. It has been hypothesized that the speech of patients with schizophrenic thought disorder may be a form of fluent aphasia, although direct support for this hypothesis is weak.

Several abnormalities of cranial nerve functioning may be seen in schizophrenia. Those most frequently found include excessive blinking (associated with increased dopaminergic activity), difficulties with smooth pursuit eye movement (SPEM), saccadic intrusions, impaired vestibular response (reduced nystagmus) on caloric stimulation of the inner ear, and impaired gag reflex.

Table 6-1: Neurologic 'Soft Signs' Frequently Seen in Schizophrenia*

Mental Status
- Attention deficits
- Denial of illness
- Speech problems
- Extinction on hand-face test
- Right-left confusion
- Perseveration, impersistence
- Bizarre responses
- Errors in cognition
- Erratic performance

Motor System
- Abnormal finger tapping performance
- Abnormal gait
- Choreoathetoid movements
- Difficulty manipulating objects
- Dysdiadochokinesia
- Hypotonia
- Mirroring phenomena

Abnormalities of motor functioning are well documented in patients with schizophrenia, including those who have never received neuroleptic medication. These may sometimes lead to further diagnostic tests because of their resemblance to signs of specific CNS diseases. (See the Cadet and Manschreck references for further information.)

Catatonic symptoms, which are listed and defined in Table 3-5, involve motor abnormalities. Other motor symptoms are often associated with formal thought disorder, speech abnormalities, and affective blunting. These include abnormal movements of all types, postural dis-

Cortical Sensory Signs
- Agraphesthesia
- Astereognosis
- Inability to localize a tactile stimulus (topognosia)

Primitive Reflexes (Frontal Lobe 'Release' Signs)
- Glabellar
- Grasp
- Palmomental
- Snout
- Suck

*Modified from Cadet JL, Rickler KC, Weinberger DR: Clinical neurologic examination. In Nasrallah HA, Weinberger DR, eds. *Handbook of Schizophrenia, Volume I: The Neurology of Schizophrenia.* New York, Elsevier, 1986.

turbances, clumsiness, repetitive movements, perseveration, delayed response, motor blocking, and lengthy completion of movements. Many of these abnormalities may be markers of neurodevelopmental CNS pathology rather than a direct consequence of schizophrenia.

Neuropsychologic Abnormalities

The science of neuropsychology originated in efforts to localize CNS lesions for diagnostic purposes by testing performance on structured mental tasks assumed to be functions of discrete neuronal centers. In recent years, the emphasis has shifted from localization to assessment of specific mental functions or abilities that are thought to be irreducible to simpler processes. Neuropsychologic testing is a tool for understanding the functioning of neural networks, for assessing their integrity, for planning and evaluating individual rehabilitation programs, and for monitoring the treatment or progression of brain diseases.

As a group, patients with schizophrenia show abnormalities, as illustrated in Figure 6-1, on virtually every neuropsychologic measure. For example, patients with schizophrenia have average IQ scores approximately 5 points lower than those of well-matched controls. This finding, described as a *generalized neurocognitive deficit,* strongly supports the association of schizophrenia with compromised brain functioning. Similar findings have been reported in patients with severe mood disorders, but deficits in the latter group are correlated with symptom intensity and often disappear or ameliorate when symptoms remit, except in a subset of patients with severe bipolar disorder.

In almost every pair of monozygotic twins discordant for schizophrenia, the affected twin functions more poorly than the healthy co-twin does. This is true even when both members of the pair score 'within normal limits' on whatever measure is studied. This observation, along with the pattern of a generalized shift in the distribution of measurements, strongly suggests that neurocognitive impairment is universal in schizophrenia and not restricted to a subgroup of patients.

Several other generalizations about the cognitive deficit of schizophrenia are widely accepted. First, it is not an artifact that can be adequately explained by poor motivation or cooperation, poor comprehension, impairment from positive symptoms, or medication. Second, although brain functioning is frequently already compromised before the onset of psychosis, suggesting a prepsychotic neurodevelopmental impairment, there is also evidence that cognitive functioning worsens in many patients at onset of psychosis. Third, cognitive impairment is not reversed by the older antipsy-

Table 6-2: Some Specific Domains of Neuropsychologic Impairment in Schizophrenia

- Continuous attention, vigilance, freedom from distractibility
- Memory (recognition, recall, verbal, and visual, but not registration, procedural, or implicit)
- Working memory (temporary storage of information being cognitively processed)
- Executive functioning (cognitive functions necessary for complex, goal-directed behavior and adaptation to environmental changes and demands, including anticipation, goal selection, considering alternatives, planning, flexibility, self-monitoring, and self-awareness)
- Language (syntactic complexity, verbal fluency)

chotic medications or by resolution of positive symptoms. Fourth, in some patients, the decline in functioning progresses for several years, although generally not indefinitely. This suggests a neurodegenerative process. Fifth, atypical antipsychotic medication may have beneficial effects that halt and perhaps even reverse cognitive impairment associated with schizophrenia. This is discussed further in Chapter 8.

There has been much debate about whether generalized cognitive impairment can be attributed to one or more core deficits that might be informative about schizophrenic pathophysiology. Table 6-2 lists some neuropsychologic domains that have been extensively studied. Some investigators argue that impairments in one or more of these domains are disproportionately frequent or severe and are therefore more central to schizophrenia. Many of these functions have been linked with activity of the dorsolateral prefrontal cortex and temporolimbic structures.

Postmortem Findings

A flurry of neuropathologic reports on schizophrenia appeared in the first half of the 20th century. Because the abnormalities reported were inconsistent and relatively minor compared with those found in other brain diseases, these findings were criticized as postmortem artifacts or variants of normal, and even as 'neuromythology.' One prominent neurologist referred to schizophrenia as 'the graveyard of neuropathologists,' indicating that new approaches were needed before any progress could be expected. This field of study then lay fallow for several decades. Improved diagnostic reliability following publication of DSM-III and the development of in vivo brain imaging procedures led to discoveries that suggested new morphometric and histologic techniques and revived interest in postmortem studies of schizophrenia.

Table 6-3 summarizes prominent findings in recent years. Important trends include: (1) Morphometric studies find diffuse changes in whole brain and tissue density, abnormalities of cortical sulci and gyri, and changes in the size of medial temporal lobe (hippocampus, amygdala, parahippocampal gyrus, entorhinal cortex) and subcortical (thalamus, basal ganglia) structures. (2) Histologic studies find architectonic abnormalities such as reductions in neuronal density and size, changes in alignment and shape, and irregularities of arrangement, positioning, and laminar distribution of neurons in medial temporal, frontal, dorsolateral prefrontal, and cingulate structures. (3) Quantitative studies of axons, dendrites, synapses, and synapse-related proteins and mRNAs suggest abnormal patterns of neuronal connection. (4) Histochemical studies have also reported regional abnormalities in neurotransmitters and their associated receptors, metabolites, substrates, and enzymes. These findings are more controversial, and consensus is not yet apparent.

Most of these abnormalities are found only in subgroups of patients, particularly in early-onset cases, and suggest

Table 6-3: Structural Brain Abnormalities in Postmortem Studies of Schizophrenia

Diffuse Abnormalities
- ↓Brain weight (by 5% to 8%) and anterior-posterior length (by about 5%)
- ↓Tissue density in cortical gray matter (but not in white matter)

Cortical Abnormalities
- Narrowing of gyri and widening of sulci
- Reversal in normal hemispheric asymmetry

Volumetric Abnormalities
- ↓Thalamus, especially dorsomedial nucleus
- ↓Amygdala
- ↓Hippocampus
- ↓Parahippocampal gyrus
- ↓Superior temporal gyrus
- ↑Basal ganglia components

Cytoarchitectonic Abnormalities
- Hippocampus
- Cingulate cortex
- Entorhinal cortex
- Dorsolateral prefrontal cortex

focal rather than general brain pathology. Their relevance for schizophrenia is attributed to their location in areas of high neuronal connectivity. Their origin is assumed to be neurodevelopmental because most studies report an absence of gliosis that would be expected if they had occurred postnatally. The usual explanatory hypothesis is that neuronal migration and differentiation were disrupted by intrauterine adverse effects of environmental or genetic origin. Some findings are still controversial because of small samples, questionable control groups, uncertainty about drug effects, and conflicting results from different laboratories. They are, however, consistent with and complementary to findings from other types of studies, particularly those described in the next section.

In Vivo CT and MRI Studies

The technologic advance that undoubtedly has had the greatest impact on schizophrenia research is the development of highly precise and minimally invasive methods of visualizing the structure and functioning of living human brains—computed tomography (CT) and magnetic resonance imaging (MRI). An early finding with this technology was that the lateral cerebral ventricles are frequently enlarged in patients with schizophrenia, usually described today as a distributional shift (increase) in the ventricle-to-brain ratio (VBR) (Figure 6-2).

Although this is arguably the most consistent and reproducible finding in pathophysiologic studies, the effect size is small, and it is neither universal nor specific to schizophrenia. It has been verified in approximately 80% of published studies. One review concluded that variations in reported differences between patients and controls were more attributable to variations within the control populations than within the patient groups. A meta-analysis concluded that the reported magnitude of the difference has declined over succeeding years, probably because of more careful selection of control subjects.

Most studies agree that increased VBR correlates with cognitive impairment, other neuropsychologic abnormalities, negative symptoms, poorer response to conventional neuroleptics, poor premorbid functioning, and chronicity.

Of possible importance for treatment selection are several studies' findings that the volume of the caudate nucleus is increased by treatment with typical neuroleptics but not by treatment with the atypical agent clozapine

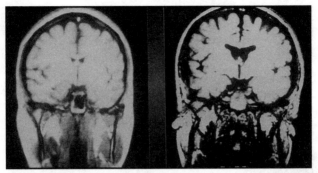

Figure 6-2: MRI scans of a healthy 25-year-old man (left) and a 25-year-old man with schizophrenia (right). Note the dilated lateral cerebral ventricles and third ventricle and the cortical sulcal widening and sylvian fissure widening in the brain of the patient with schizophrenia.

(Clozaril®) and that caudate volume decreases when patients are switched from a traditional neuroleptic to clozapine or, possibly, to another atypical antipsychotic. Thalamic size, which is often subnormal in schizophrenia, has also been shown to increase with treatment by typical or atypical antipsychotics.

Although methodology and imaging technology have advanced considerably, structural neuroimaging research is still complicated by factors such as patient characteristics (age, sex, health status, chronicity of illness, previous treatment, institutional residence), drug effects, control subject characteristics, differences in scanning technique, and uncertainty in locating anatomic landmarks.

Table 6-4 summarizes findings reported in nearly 200 MRI studies published between 1988 and 2000. Buckley has suggested that the following trends are evident in this literature: (1) Structural abnormalities are more pronounced in male patients than in female patients. (2) Abnormalities may show a predilection for the left hemisphere. (3) Temporal lobe abnormalities are correlated with positive symp-

Table 6-4: Structural Brain Abnormalities Found In Vivo in CT and MRI Studies of Schizophrenia*

Cortical

- Widened fissures and sulci (especially sylvian and interhemispheric)
- Abnormal sulcal-gyral configurations
- ↓Cranial volume
- ↓Gray matter volume
- ↓Gray matter density (especially in anterior left hemisphere)
- ↓Brain tissue volume
- ↓Frontal volume
- ↓Temporal volume
- ↓Parietal volume
- ↓Inferior parietal lobule volume
- Abnormal hemispheric asymmetries

Limbic System (may be more pronounced in left hemisphere)

- ↓Hippocampus volume
- ↓Amygdala volume
- ↓Parahippocampal gyrus volume
- ↓Olfactory bulb volume
- Abnormal sulcal-gyral configuration in entorhinal cortex

toms. (4) Studies of high-risk families show a pattern of abnormalities in relatives that is similar to, but less pronounced than, the pattern seen in patients. (5) In monozygotic twin pairs discordant for schizophrenia, affected twins show more ventricular enlargement and more temporal lobe abnormalities than their nonaffected co-twins.

Subcortical

- ↑Ventricle-to-brain ratio (VBR)
- ↑Lateral ventricular volume
- ↑Temporal horn of the lateral ventricles
- ↑Third ventricular volume
- ↑Caudate nucleus volume (probably caused by conventional neuroleptic treatment)
- ↓Thalamic volume (may be reversed by antipsychotic treatment)
- ↑Thickness of corpus callosum
- ↑Length of corpus callosum
- ↑Frequency of cavum septum pellucidum

Other

- ↓Volume of midline cerebellar structures (vermis)
- Gray matter heterotopias
- Unidentified bright objects (UBOs), probably related to microvascular ischemia

*Modified from Nasrallah HA: Relationship of structural brain changes to antipsychotic drug response in schizophrenia. In Shriqui CL, Nasrallah HA, eds. *Contemporary Issues in the Treatment of Schizophrenia.* Washington, DC, American Psychiatric Press, 1995:209-224.

Although it was once thought that these deficits were nonprogressive and predated the onset of psychosis, perhaps by many years, more recent studies have found a subgroup of patients who show progressive ventricular enlargement during the first few years of illness. This finding raises the possibility that a secondary neurodegenerative process is superimposed on the 'static enceph-alopathy' that is assumed to be neurodevelopmental in origin. One hypothesis is that positive (psychotic) symptoms are concurrent with neurotoxic degeneration and that the latter may be associated with a marked increase in catecholamine activity. This seems compatible with the finding that negative symptoms and cognitive impairment worsen over time in many patients and eventually reach a plateau, while psychotic symptoms tend to become less prominent. Perhaps antipsychotic medication blocks the neurotoxic process. This would explain the finding that the duration of untreated psychotic symptoms during the early stage of psychosis may correlate with long-term outcome.

In Vivo Imaging of Brain Function

Positron emission tomography (PET) and single photon emission computed tomography (SPECT) are capable of displaying localized measurement of regional cerebral blood flow (rCBF) and regional cerebral glucose metabolism (rCGM). When these techniques were first applied to the study of patients with schizophrenia, a frequently reported finding was a deficit in metabolic activity in frontal areas relative to postcentral regions. This finding was termed *hypofrontality* and was interpreted as evidence of frontal lobe pathology in schizophrenia. Hypofrontality was confirmed by several subsequent studies and disconfirmed by others. It appeared that hypofrontality was more frequent in chronic than in acutely ill patients. Clearly, patient characteristics had to be controlled more carefully before consistent replication could be achieved. Since that time, new strategies have produced results that can be confirmed in other laboratories.

In the *activation strategy,* patients are compared with controls during performance of a specific mental task. In the prototypic activation study, Weinberger et al measured rCBF while testing patients and controls with the Wisconsin Card Sorting Test (WCST), a measure of executive functioning. It is known that a good WCST performance depends on intact dorsolateral frontal lobe functioning and that patients with schizophrenia perform poorly on the WCST. Weinberger et al found consistent large increases in frontal rCBF in control subjects during the WCST, compared with a resting state, but patients showed a wide range of changes, including blunted or absent increases and even decreases. In patients, there was a strong correlation of frontal rCBF with WCST performance, suggesting that ability to activate the frontal cortex was the limiting factor that determined performance.

Subsequent studies by the same authors showed that the impaired frontal function was independent of medication and of factors such as attention and positive symptoms. A study of monozygotic twin pairs discordant for schizophrenia found that affected twins consistently showed less frontal activation than their co-twins during the WCST. Another study reported a correlation of diminished prefrontal activation during the WCST with decreased hippocampal volume.

Blood flow imaging technology can also identify symptom-specific patterns of abnormality. A prominent example is the work of Liddle et al, who found specific rCBF patterns that correlated with symptoms of reality distortion, disorganization, and psychomotor poverty. Their major findings, which have been largely confirmed in several other laboratories, are summarized in Table 6-5.

Another application of PET technology is in vivo imaging of neurotransmitter receptors. Receptor-imaging studies have strongly confirmed the link of neuroleptic efficacy with D_2 receptor blockade and identified the therapeutic range of receptor occupancy required (60% to 65% for conventional neuroleptics). They have also found that occupancy of more than 80% of nigrostriatal DA receptors is strongly associated with extrapyramidal side effects (EPS).

Some atypical antipsychotics bind with fewer D_2 receptors in nigrostriatal systems than in mesolimbic DA sys-

Table 6-5: Abnormalities of rCBF Associated With Three Dimensions of Schizophrenic Symptoms*

Reality Distortion Dimension (hallucinations and delusions)
- ↑In left medial temporal lobe (including parahippocampal gyrus, ventral striatum, and inferolateral prefrontal cortex)
- ↓In posterior cingulate cortex
- ↓In left lateral temporoparietal cortex

Disorganization Dimension (eg, thought disorder, inappropriate affect)
- ↑In anterior cingulate cortex
- ↑In thalamus
- ↓In ventrolateral prefrontal cortex and contiguous insula
- ↓In parietal association cortex

Psychomotor Poverty Syndrome (eg, poverty of speech, flat affect, decreased movement)
- ↓In lateral prefrontal cortex
- ↓In parietal association cortex
- ↑In caudate nuclei

rCBF = regional cerebral blood flow

*From Liddle PF: The multidimensional phenotype of schizophrenia. In: Tamminga CA, ed. *Schizophrenia in a Molecular Age*. Washington, DC, American Psychiatric Press, 1999. Oldham JA, Riba MB, eds. *Review of Psychiatry*; vol 18.

tems. They also achieve their therapeutic effects with a lower proportion of mesolimbic D_2 receptor occupancy. These findings help to explain the lower frequency of EPS with atypical antipsychotics.

Other in vivo imaging technologies used in schizophrenia research include magnetic resonance spectroscopy (MRS), functional magnetic resonance imaging (fMRI), and brain electrical activity mapping (BEAM).

MRS provides measurements of various neurochemicals within a volume of brain tissue selected by the investigator in a specified brain region. Odd-numbered nuclei, which are paramagnetic, enable the generation of a spectrum of resonances for compounds containing that particular nucleus. The most widely used nuclei in MRS research in schizophrenia are hydrogen (^{1}H) and phosphorus (^{31}P). Proton MRS research over the past decade has produced some important findings. First, there is a reduction of N-acetyl-aspartate (NAA) in the hippocampus of patients with schizophrenia, which implies the loss of neurons because NAA is considered a neuronal marker. The initial study of Nasrallah et al (1994) has been replicated by several other groups, and decreases of NAA in the frontal lobe have also been reported. Second, phosphomonoester is decreased and phosphodiester is increased in the frontal lobe. These changes have implications for neurodevelopmental synaptic pruning during childhood and adolescence in schizophrenia.

fMRI is a noninvasive method of mapping brain tissue activation in response to a wide variety of external stimuli (eg, visual, auditory, somatosensory) and internal stimuli (eg, hallucinations, mood change). This relatively new field of research is already demonstrating significant deviations in cerebral organization and activation in the brains of persons with schizophrenia.

Quantitative electroencephalography (EEG), also known as BEAM, enables researchers to visualize changes in brain electrical activity that is transformed into color-coded maps. It is a useful tool for comparing patients with schizophrenia to other groups and for studying the effect of stimuli or medications on regional brain electrical activity.

Psychophysiologic Abnormalities

There are two reasons for studying psychophysiologic abnormalities linked to schizophrenia. First, such abnormalities may help in identifying specific brain circuits affected by the disease. Second, these abnormalities may be trait markers that correlate with genetic vulnerability for schizophrenia. Two psychophysiologic abnormalities that have been frequently studied are impairment of SPEM while tracking a moving target and abnormal event-related potentials (ERPs).

Eye Tracking Movements

Eye tracking abnormalities associated with schizophrenia have been reported for nearly a century. In modern studies the subject is asked to keep his or her gaze fixed as closely as possible on a moving target, such as a pendulum swinging or an image on a video screen. Task performance is monitored by recording eye movements, either with an electro-oculograph or by reflecting infrared light from the pupil. Methods of evaluating performance range from impressionistic ratings by examiners (presumably blinded to diagnosis) to various quantitative methods. Examples of normal and deviant performance are shown in Figure 6-3.

Patients with schizophrenia show greatly elevated rates of SPEM abnormalities (reports range from 20% to 80%) compared with normal control subjects (about 8%). Some studies report that patients with bipolar disorder also show abnormalities but less frequently than patients with schizophrenia. Types of abnormality reported include low-gain (low-velocity) pursuit, saccadic tracking, saccadic intrusions, and velocity arrests. Although interventions that help the subject focus attention can improve performance, the deviations cannot be entirely explained as resulting from attentional impairment, poor cooperation, or medication. Abnormalities precede the onset of psychosis and persist continuously, even when the patient is psychiatrically well.

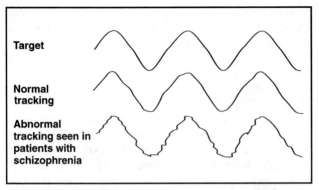

Figure 6-3: Smooth pursuit eye movements. The bottom is typical of those produced by many patients with schizophrenia. From Levy DL, Holzman PS, Matthysse S, et al: Eye tracking dysfunction and schizophrenia: a selective review. *Schizophr Bull* 1993;19:461-536.

The neural circuitry involved in SPEM is complex and widely distributed, including the frontal eye fields, temporal lobes, thalamus, occipital lobes, basal ganglia, cerebellum, and brainstem. Abnormal SPEM has been shown to be genetically determined. In twin studies, correlations of SPEM parameters are much higher in monozygotic twin pairs than in dizygotic twin pairs. About 50% of first-degree relatives of patients with schizophrenia show similar abnormalities, including relatives who show no overt signs of schizophrenia spectrum disease. Curiously, some probands with normal SPEM have close relatives with abnormal SPEM. One hypothesis to explain this finding is that abnormal SPEM is a 'latent trait marker' of high genetic diathesis for schizophrenia.

Event-Related Potentials

ERPs are electrical waveforms generated in brainstem structures in response to external stimuli. The typical study paradigm involves scalp electroencephalogram recording during repeated presentations of stimuli. Electrical responses are averaged over many trials to produce a smooth waveform with measurable parameters. Shifts between negative and positive voltage occur at characteristic times that correspond with the mental processing of the stimulus as it passes through neural networks.

One ERP waveform frequently studied in schizophrenia is the P300. To assess P300, a subject is fitted with earphones and instructed to count the number of infrequent high-pitched tones embedded randomly in a sequence of low-pitched tones. The P300 is a positive peak occurring about 300 milliseconds (ms) (between 200 and 500 ms) after an unexpected or surprising stimulus (the high-pitched tone). Its relatively long latency indicates that complex cognitive processing has taken place. The amplitude of response is interpreted as the degree of surprise and the latency as the time required for information processing. About 50% of patients with schizophrenia show either reduced amplitude or delayed latency (by about 50 ms) compared with control subjects. These abnormalities are interpreted as impairment of information processing.

P300 abnormalities occur much more frequently in first-degree relatives of patients than in relatives of controls. Subjects with schizotypal personality have P300 abnormalities greater than those of controls but less than those of patients with schizophrenia.

Neuropharmacology of Schizophrenia

This section summarizes some neuropharmacologic mechanisms of dopamine and serotonin that are believed to be important in the pathophysiology or treatment of schizophrenia.

Dopamine

Chlorpromazine (Thorazine®) was originally tested in humans for its strong antihistaminic properties and was soon used for its calming effects in surgical patients. When tried in psychotic patients, it was found to have the unexpected ability to reduce core psychotic symptoms (hallucinations, delusions, and agitation) without a corresponding reduction in the level of consciousness. As the first antipsychotic drug, it was soon in widespread use in asylums throughout the world. (The weaker antipsychotic action of reserpine, a depleter of DA and other monoamines, was discovered at about the same time. Side effects limited and eventually ended reserpine's use in psychiatry.)

A frequent side effect of chlorpromazine was a parkinsonian syndrome, which was found to be fully reversible by stopping the drug. Trials of the drug in laboratory animals identified a characteristic profile of behavioral effects, including the syndrome of *neurolepsis,* characterized by absence or extreme slowness of motor activity and behavioral indifference to normally arousing stimuli. In humans, neurolepsis consists of bradykinesia (slowed and reduced movements) and emotional calming. Neurolepsis, parkinsonism, and antipsychotic efficacy were strongly linked with DA antagonism.

As a result of these findings, ability to induce neurolepsis in laboratory animals became a screening criterion in the search for similar compounds. The drugs developed by this method are known as *neuroleptics* or *typical antipsychotics*.

The *dopamine hypothesis of schizophrenia* proposed that excessive DA function is intrinsic to the pathophysiology of schizophrenia. This hypothesis was initially supported by two types of indirect evidence: (1) the link between DA antagonism and the therapeutic efficacy of chlorpromazine and similar drugs and (2) the observation that DA agonist drugs such as amphetamine and cocaine quickly worsen psychotic symptoms in schizophrenia and can induce psychotic syndromes during prolonged or excessive use in persons who do not have schizophrenia. It was reinforced by many further findings in studies of neuroleptic drugs. The strongest evidence against the DA hypothesis has been the 30% of patients who respond poorly (or not at all) to neuroleptics.

Although simplistic efforts to explain schizophrenia by abnormality of a single neurotransmitter are no longer viable, carefully qualified versions of the DA hypothesis are still important in schizophrenia research today. One working model that has emerged suggests that DA may be increased in subcortical regions and decreased in the frontal cortex.

In the CNS, DA is synthesized from tyrosine; an intermediate metabolic product is levodopa. DA is also the immediate precursor in the biosynthesis of norepinephrine, another neurotransmitter.

There are four major DA systems in the brain. Three of them have cell bodies located in the ventral tegmental area of the mesencephalon. The *nigrostriatal DA system* has projections to the basal ganglia. The *mesolimbic DA system* projects to nuclei in the limbic system. The *mesocortical DA system* projects to the cerebral cortex, especially the limbic and frontal cortices. The *tuberoinfundibular DA system* is entirely contained within the hypothalamus. Hypothalamic DA is released into the hypothalamic-hypophyseal venous system and transported to the anterior pituitary, where it binds with D_2 receptors on lactotrophs, thereby inhibiting secretion of prolactin. Certain neuroleptic side effects, especially galactorrhea, gynecomastia, and amenorrhea, result from disinhibition of prolactin secretion.

Positive psychotic symptoms that respond to neuroleptic therapy are assumed to result from excessive mesolimbic DA activity. Considerable evidence supports the belief that all therapeutic effects of neuroleptic drugs are obtained by mesolimbic and possibly mesocortical DA antagonism.

The acute EPS of neuroleptics (parkinsonism and other abnormal movement disorders such as akathisia and acute dystonic reactions) are caused by excessive DA antagonism in the nigrostriatal DA system. Another group of drug-induced movement disorders, called *tardive dyskinesias* (more properly, *tardive movement disorders*), develop slowly during a long period of neuroleptic use and may progress to irreversibility if neuroleptic treatment continues, especially if dosage is excessively high. Tardive dyskinesias are believed to be caused by *denervation supersensitivity* of nigrostriatal DA receptors, which produces compensatory upregulation of their density, as evidenced by increased volume of the caudate nucleus.

Negative symptoms and the deficit syndrome of schizophrenia are believed to be associated with reduced DA function in the mesocortical system, especially in the frontal lobe. This explains why neuroleptic drugs can themselves cause or worsen negative symptoms. Whether cognitive impairment is also linked with mesocortical DA inhibition is under debate.

Many types of DA receptors exist in the CNS. Five subtypes of interest are known as D_1 through D_5. Overwhelming evidence links the therapeutic action of traditional neuroleptics with antagonism of the D_2 receptor, which is found in all four of the DA systems listed above.

DA neurons in the mesolimbic and nigrostriatal systems also have presynaptic autoreceptors that regulate DA synthesis and release. These autoreceptors are the D_2 subtype and therefore are blocked by neuroleptics. The result is a counterproductive increase in presynaptic DA release by the same mechanism that causes postsynaptic therapeutic effects. DA agonists that bind selectively with presynaptic receptors reduce positive symptoms by a mechanism fundamentally different from all other antipsychotics, old or new. An example is aripiprazole (Abilitat®), a partial DA agonist that stabilizes receptor function, normalizing both overactive and underactive DA systems.

Atypical antipsychotics differ in important ways from traditional neuroleptics. The prototype of this group is clozapine, which was first synthesized in 1959 and is therefore an older drug. It was not marketed in the United States until 1989 because of its high toxicity. Compared with chlorpromazine, clozapine is more anticholinergic, is more sedating, is more likely to cause seizures and weight gain, and has an approximate 1% risk of life-threatening agranulocytosis.

However, clozapine also has advantages compared with chlorpromazine. It was long known to have extremely low potential for causing acute EPS and to not cause hyper-prolactinemia or tardive dyskinesia. The US Food and Drug Administration (FDA) finally granted approval for its use because of convincing evidence that it is more effective than typical antipsychotics for refractory positive symptoms. In particular, clozapine produces significant improvement in at least half of all patients who respond poorly to neuroleptics. Also, it may actually improve some negative symptoms, and it may reduce neurocognitive impairment caused by schizophrenia or associated with excessive D_2 blockade.

Like clozapine, other fully atypical antipsychotics (ie, atypical at all doses) cause minimal acute EPS and do not increase prolactin secretion. They also do not cause or worsen negative symptoms, and they may lessen cognitive impairment. Because they are relatively new drugs, they have not yet been convincingly shown to not cause tardive dyskinesia. No other drug, typical or atypical, has been shown to equal clozapine in overall therapeutic efficacy for treatment-resistant or refractory schizophrenia.

Compared with typical antipsychotics, some of clozapine's advantages are explained by differences in its actions in the DA system. First, it has lower binding affinity for D_2 receptors. Second, it binds more readily with mesolimbic D_2 receptors than with mesocortical, nigrostriatal, and tuberoinfundibular receptors. Third, PET studies show that a lower proportion of mesolimbic D_2 receptor occupancy is required for therapeutic efficacy. Clozapine also has high binding affinity for D_1 and D_4 receptors, although the significance of this is uncertain. Similar properties have also been verified for several other atypical antipsychotics.

Another important difference between typical and atypical antipsychotics is the distinctive effects of the latter in brain serotonergic systems.

Serotonin and Atypical Antipsychotics

Some of the benefits of clozapine and other atypical antipsychotics have been linked with their high affinity for serotonin 5-HT_{2A} receptors. Traditional neuroleptics do not have comparable effects on these receptors.

Nigrostriatal DA neurons contain 5-HT_{2A} receptors; the effect of serotonin is to inhibit release of nigrostriatal DA. Thus, blockade of these 5-HT_{2A} receptors counteracts the effects of D_2 receptor blockade and promotes DA release. This competitively reduces the D_2-blocking action of the atypical antipsychotic—in the region where D_2 blockade is not desirable—resulting in lower nigrostriatal D_2 receptor occupancy and fewer EPS.

Similarly, atypical drugs promote DA release in the mesocortical system. Here, 5-HT_{2A} receptors are more abundant than D_2 receptors, producing a net increase in mesocortical DA activity despite the blockade of some D_2 receptors. This counteracts negative, mood, and cognitive symptoms caused by DA deficiency and receptor blockade.

In the tuberoinfundibular system, serotonin promotes and dopamine inhibits prolactin release. Simultaneous blockade of 5-HT_{2A} and D_2 receptors in this region results in little net change in prolactin secretion rather than the hyperprolactinemia caused by D_2 blockade alone.

Neurodevelopmental and Neurodegenerative Processes in Schizophrenia

Because of Kraepelin's emphasis on progression, deterioration, and dementia, early hypotheses about the pathogenesis of schizophrenia involved cerebral degeneration. The failure of neuropathologic studies to produce consistent and convincing evidence of degeneration in most patients, along with Bleuler's suggestion that mild cases might not involve cerebral disease, caused interest to shift from biologic to psychologic theories. These hypotheses predominated, particularly in the United States, until the 1960s.

The modern era of schizophrenia research has produced compelling evidence that brain function is abnormal, that brain structure is altered in many patients—especially those with more severe illness—and that a genetic predisposition is important. Chapter 5 describes a large body of research demonstrating that a variety of neurodevelopmental (perinatal and obstetric) mishaps increase the risk for schizophrenia in persons who have the necessary genetic diathesis. This led to the 'hit and run' hypothesis that a genetically predisposed brain is prepared for schizophrenia during early development, perhaps during critical processes such as neuronal differentiation, neuronal migration, synapse formation, or synapse pruning.

Interest in neurodevelopmental hypotheses was bolstered by progress in molecular neuroembryology. Advances in neurohistologic technique demonstrated structural brain defects that appear to document prenatal insult and may help explain various features of schizophrenia. Until recently, many investigators believed that schizophrenia is a 'static encephalopathy' that originates early in development and is fully expressed only under certain conditions (a 'second hit') and usually only after brain maturation is complete (ie, in adolescence or early adulthood).

The problem with the static encephalopathy hypothesis is that it fails to explain some old and new knowledge about schizophrenia. Features such as the unpredictable clinical course, the extreme variability in outcome, the progression from predominantly positive to predominantly negative symptoms, the characteristics of the neurocognitive deficit, the beneficial effects of early drug treatment on long-term outcome, and the tendency for most cases to reach a plateau after several years of progression (suggesting a 'burnout') all suggest some sort of neurodegenerative process superimposed on faulty neurodevelopmental foundations. It is hypothesized that atypical (new) antipsychotics may have neuroprotective effects that block neurodegeneration.

Suggested Readings

Buckley PF: Structural brain imaging in schizophrenia. *Psychiatr Clin North Am* 1998;21:77-92.

Cadet JL, Rockler KC, Weinberger DR: The clinical neurologic examination in schizophrenia. In Nasrallah HA, Weinberger DR, eds. *Handbook of Schizophrenia, Volume 1: The Neurology of Schizophrenia*. New York, Elsevier, 1986:1-47.

Clardy JA, Hyde TM, Kleinman JE: Postmortem neurochemical and neuropathological studies in schizophrenia. In Andreasen NC, ed. *Schizophrenia: From Mind to Molecule*. Washington, DC, American Psychiatric Press, 1994:123-146.

Dwork AJ: Postmortem studies of the hippocampal formation in schizophrenia. *Schizophr Bull* 1997;23:385-402.

Falkai P, Bogerts B: The neuropathology of schizophrenia. In Hirsch SR, Weinberger DR, eds. *Schizophrenia*. Oxford, Blackwell Science Ltd, 1995:275-292.

Friedman D: Endogenous scalp-recorded brain potentials in schizophrenia: a methodological review. In Steinhauer SR, Gruzelier JH, Zubin J, eds. *Handbook of Schizophrenia, Volume 5: Neuropsychology, Psychophysiology, and Information Processing*. Amsterdam, Elsevier, 1991:91-127.

Goldberg TE, Gold JM: Neurocognitive deficits in schizophrenia. In Hirsch SR, Weinberger DR, eds. *Schizophrenia*. Oxford, Blackwell Science Ltd, 1995:146-162.

Heckers S: Neuropathology of schizophrenia: cortex, thalamus, basal ganglia, and neurotransmitter-specific projection systems. *Schizophr Bull* 1997;23:403-421.

Heinrichs RW: *In Search of Madness: Schizophrenia and Neuroscience*. Oxford, Oxford University Press, 2001.

Hoff AL: Neuropsychological function in schizophrenia. In Shriqui CL, Nasrallah HA, eds. *Contemporary Issues in the Treatment of Schizophrenia*. Washington, DC, American Psychiatric Press, 1995:187-208.

Holzman PS: Eye movement dysfunctions in schizophrenia. In Steinhauer SR, Gruzelier JH, Zubin J, eds. *Handbook of Schizo-*

phrenia, Volume 5: Neuropsychology, Psychophysiology, and Information Processing. Amsterdam, Elsevier, 1991:129-145.

Liddle PF: Brain imaging. In Hirsch SR, Weinberger DR, eds. *Schizophrenia.* Oxford, Blackwell Science Ltd, 1995:425-442.

Liddle PF: The multidimensional phenotype of schizophrenia. In Tamminga CA, ed. *Schizophrenia in a Molecular Age.* Washington, DC, American Psychiatric Press; 1999:1-28. Oldham JA, Riba MB, eds. *Review of Psychiatry*; vol 18.

Lidow MS, ed. *Neurotransmitter Receptors in Actions of Antipsychotic Medications.* Boca Raton, FL, CRC Press, 2000.

Manschreck TC: Motor abnormalities in schizophrenic disorders. In Nasrallah HA, Weinberger DR, eds. *Handbook of Schizophrenia, Volume I: The Neurology of Schizophrenia.* New York, Elsevier, 1986:65-96.

McClure RJ, Keshavan MS, Pettegrew JW: Chemical and physiologic brain imaging in schizophrenia. *Psychiatr Clin North Am* 1998;21:93-122.

Nasrallah HA: Neurodevelopmental pathogenesis of schizophrenia. *Psychiatr Clin North Am* 1993;16:269-280.

Nasrallah HA: Relationship of structural brain changes to antipsychotic drug response in schizophrenia. In Shriqui CL, Nasrallah HA, eds. *Contemporary Issues in the Treatment of Schizophrenia.* Washington, DC, American Psychiatric Press, 1995:209-224.

Nasrallah HA, Skinner TE, Schmalbrock P, et al: Proton magnetic resonance spectroscopy (^{1}H MRS) of the hippocampal formation in schizophrenia: a pilot study. *Br J Psychiatry* 1994;165:481-485.

Nasrallah HA, Wilcox JA: Gender differences in the etiology and symptoms of schizophrenia: brain injury versus genetic factors. *Ann Clin Psychiatry* 1989;1:51-53.

Sharma T, Harvey P: *Cognition in Schizophrenia.* Oxford, Oxford University Press, 2000.

Shenton ME, Dickey CC, Frumin M, et al: A review of MRI findings in schizophrenia. *Schizophr Res* 2001;49:1-52.

Stahl SM: *Essential Psychopharmacology: Neuroscientific Basis and Practical Applications.* 2nd ed. Cambridge, Cambridge University Press, 2000.

Straube ER, Oades RD: *Schizophrenia: Empirical Research and Findings.* San Diego, Academic Press, 1992.

Waddington JL, Lane A, Scully PJ, et al: Neurodevelopmental and neuroprogressive processes in schizophrenia: antithetical or complementary, over a lifetime trajectory of disease? *Psychiatr Clin North Am* 1998;21:123-149.

Chapter 7

The First-Generation Antipsychotics

The discovery of pharmacologic treatments for schizophrenia and other psychoses is one of the most remarkable chapters in the history of medicine. The process of discovery was as serendipitous as the discovery of penicillin and just as welcome for the millions of individuals with psychotic brain disorders who were doomed to spend their lives sequestered in 'insane asylums,' receiving ineffectual treatments such as hydrotherapy and 'spinning chairs.' The advent of medications that could suppress delusions, hallucinations, abnormal thoughts, and bizarre behavior helped to demystify mental illness and portray it as a medical illness and to reduce the stigma associated with illnesses such as schizophrenia. Antipsychotics also triggered intensive neuroscience research into brain structure and function in all psychiatric disorders.

The first-generation antipsychotics, starting with chlorpromazine (Thorazine®) in the early 1950s, were used for more than 4 decades, until the advent of the new second-generation antipsychotics in the mid-1990s. The new antipsychotics have rapidly supplanted the first-generation antipsychotics and have become the standard of care. This chapter reviews the first-generation antipsychotics and highlights the reasons most practitioners have switched most patients to the new antipsychotics. The discussion of first-generation antipsychotics focuses on limitations

Table 7-1: Classes of the First-Generation Antipsychotics

Class	Representative Drug (Brand Name)
Phenothiazines	
Aliphatic	chlorpromazine (Thorazine®)
Piperazine	trifluoperazine (Stelazine®)
Piperidine	thioridazine (Mellaril®)
Butyrophenones	haloperidol (Haldol®)
Thioxanthines	thiothixene (Navane®)
Dibenzoxazepines	loxapine (Loxitane®)
Dihydroindolones	molindone (Moban®)
Diphenylbutylpiperidine	pimozide (Orap®)

in their efficacy and safety and sets the stage for a detailed discussion of the new antipsychotics and their uses in the next chapter.

The First-Generation Antipsychotics

Members of this class are also referred to as major tranquilizers, neuroleptics, typical antipsychotics, or conventional antipsychotics.

After the accidental discovery in the early 1950s in Europe that the antihistamine chlorpromazine, a phenothiazine, also exerts antipsychotic effects, pharmaceutical companies synthesized numerous related phenothiazines through side-chain substitutions. In all, six classes of first-generation antipsychotics were developed between 1952 and 1975 (Table 7-1). Thirteen first-generation antipsychotics are still available in the United States, although their use has now dwindled to less than 10% of patients. Several more first-generation antipsychotics are available in Europe and the rest of the world. After decades of use, there is little evidence that first-generation antipsychotics have any efficacy differences among them, although they do differ in their side-effect profiles.

Mechanism of Action

Initially, the mechanism of action of the first-generation antipsychotics was unknown. It soon became apparent that sedation, which occurred immediately with chlorpromazine, had little to do with the drug's antipsychotic effects, which usually occurred 3 to 6 weeks later. Subsequently, the extrapyramidal side effects (EPS) of the first-generation antipsychotics, especially pseudoparkinsonism, offered the major clue that postsynaptic dopamine receptor antagonism (most likely in the mesolimbic and mesocortical tracts) was probably the antipsychotic mechanism of action. Unfortunately, a dogma emerged in the 1960s that antipsychotic efficacy would not be achieved until EPS occurred, which is now recognized as a fallacious and dangerous assumption. Recent dopamine receptor occupancy research using positron emission tomography (PET), discussed in the next chapter, suggests that about 65% to 70% dopamine type 2 (D_2) receptor occupancy may be sufficient for antipsychotic effects. EPS emerge with excessive D_2 occupancy (80% or higher). Therefore, most patients received higher doses of first-generation antipsychotics than they needed. Moreover, the widely used anticholinergic medications (Table 7-2) that were given with the first-generation antipsychotics (often prophylactically) would not have been needed had the antipsychotics been dosed appropriately.

Clozapine (Clozaril®), a dibenzodiazepine synthesized in 1959, was regarded as 'atypical' because it exerted its antipsychotic effects without EPS, regardless of dose. The second-generation antipsychotics were modeled after clozapine's receptor affinity profile (low D_2 and higher serotonin 5-HT$_2$ blockage) in a successful effort to minimize EPS. The mechanism for this atypicality is discussed in the next chapter.

Pharmacology

Table 7-3 lists the first-generation antipsychotics with their daily dose and formulations (oral tablet, liquid suspension, intramuscular/intravenous injection, and depot, long-acting intramuscular form). Most of the first-generation antipsychotics have an elimination half-life of 16 to 45 hours (although slow and fast metabolizers in various ethnic and genetic pools may influence the elimination half-life). Most first-generation antipsychotics are metabolized (demethylated or hydroxylated) in the liver and excreted by the kidneys and gastrointestinal tract.

The parenteral forms of first-generation antipsychotics are rapidly absorbed and usually start showing their clinical effects within 10 to 15 minutes. Although not officially approved, intravenous administration of haloperidol (Haldol®) is frequently used in intensive care units for agitation or delirium. Reports of serious Q-Tc prolongation, torsades de pointes, and death have been reported with intravenous but not with oral haloperidol, possibly associated with the higher serum concentration achieved with parenteral administration, caused by circumventing the first pass through the liver.

Some depot (or long-acting) preparations of first-generation antipsychotics were synthesized by esterification of their hydroxyl moeity to an enanthate or decanoate ester. The longer half-life of the decanoate preparations fluphenazine (Prolixin®) and haloperidol, ranging between 2 and 6 weeks, enabled practitioners to treat noncompliant patients with an intramuscular injection every 2 to 4 weeks. More than 11 long-acting first-generation antipsychotics are available in Canada and Europe, including oral forms. The depot forms of the first-generation antipsychotics have remained in use for extremely noncompliant patients despite the widespread use of the oral forms of the new antipsychotics, discussed later. It should be emphasized

Table 7-2: Drugs Used for Treating Acute Extrapyramidal Side Effects of the First-Generation Antipsychotics

Generic Name	Brand Name
Anticholinergics	
benztropine	Cogentin®
biperiden	Akineton®
procyclidine	Kemadrin®
trihexyphenidyl	Artane®
diphenhydramine	Benadryl®
Benzodiazepines	
lorazepam	Ativan®
diazepam	Valium®
β-blockers	
propanolol	Inderal®
Dopamine Agonists	
amantadine	Symmetrel®
bromocriptine	Parlodel®

that poor adherence to treatment is prevalent in schizo-phrenia and accounts for most relapses. Long-acting forms of new antipsychotics have been developed and will be available soon (see Chapter 8).

In general, the first-generation antipsychotics are highly protein bound, which must be taken into account when patients concomitantly receive other drugs that are highly protein bound, because displacement would increase

Daily Dose Range (mg)	Available Formulations	
	Oral	IM
1-6	yes	yes
2-8	yes	yes
2.5-10	yes	no
2-16	yes	no
25-200	yes	yes
1-6	yes	yes
5-15	yes	yes
20-160	yes	yes
100-400	yes	no
2.5-10	yes	no

concentrations of both. Also, because of their lipophilic properties, first-generation antipsychotics achieve high concentrations in brain tissue. Studies indicate that traces of first-generation antipsychotics are detectable in brain tissue a year or more after discontinuation of the drug.

Despite an extensive number of studies on serum concentrations and clinical response, no reliable guidelines

Table 7-3: Dosage and Formulations of the Commonly Used First-Generation Antipsychotics

Antipsychotic	Daily Oral Dose Range (mg)	Oral	IM PRN	IM Depot
chlorpromazine (Thorazine®)	200-1,500	yes	yes	no
fluphenazine (Prolixin®)	2-20	yes	yes	yes
haloperidol (Haldol®)	2-20	yes	yes	yes
loxapine (Loxitane®)	20-200	yes	yes	no
mesoridazine (Serentil®)	50-400	yes	yes	no
molindone (Moban®)	20-150	yes	no	no
perphenazine	4-48	yes	yes	no
thioridazine (Mellaril®)	200-800	yes	no	no
trifluoperazine (Stelazine®)	5-50	yes	yes	no

have emerged for therapeutic serum levels or therapeutic windows for first-generation antipsychotics. One explanation is the multitude of active and inactive metabolites. A more recent explanation is that transient occupancy of D_2 receptors at the 65% level or higher may suffice for antipsychotic effects following an oral daily dose and that sustained serum concentrations may not be necessary for clinical response (discussed in Chapter 8).

Indications/Efficacy

When the first-generation antipsychotics were introduced in the 1950s, there were no regulatory US Food and Drug Administration (FDA) procedures to establish 'official' indications. Not surprisingly, the first-generation antipsychotics were used for any psychotic illness (eg, schizophrenia, schizoaffective disorder, mania, psychotic depression, brief reactive psychosis, psychosis secondary to a medical condition). They were also used in a wide range of nonpsychotic disorders such as anxiety and panic attacks, depression, agitation, insomnia, obsessive-compulsive disorder, and severe personality disorder. However, the EPS of the first-generation antipsychotics eventually limited their use to schizophrenia and other psychoses in adults, children, and the elderly. Nonpsychiatric indications for first-generation antipsychotics include treatment of emesis and certain movement disorders.

Within a decade, the efficacy of first-generation antipsychotics in schizophrenia was found to be limited. When they were discovered to suppress delusions and hallucinations, it was believed that the first-generation antipsychotics would 'cure' schizophrenia. However, clinicians and researchers soon realized that the first-generation antipsychotics had minimal, if any, efficacy on the other domains of schizophrenia, which include negative symptoms, cognitive deficits, and comorbid conditions, most commonly depression, anxiety, and substance abuse (*any* nonpsychotic axis I or axis II disorder can be comorbid with schizophrenia). In fact, the first-generation antipsychotics seemed to worsen negative, cognitive, and dysphoric symptoms in patients with schizophrenia when they were used in doses high enough to cause parkinsonism, especially in elderly patients in nursing homes with agitation or psychosis secondary to dementia.

Side Effects of First-Generation Antipsychotics

The effectiveness of a drug is a combination of its efficacy in treating symptoms and the ability of patients to tolerate its side effects. The older antipsychotics failed on both counts, but their intolerable side effects, particularly EPS, are probably the major reason for their ineffectiveness because of the reluctance of most patients to adhere to treatment. The acute and long-term movement disorders produced by first-generation antipsychotics at commonly used therapeutic doses represent serious iatrogenic brain disorders such as dystonia, akathisia, parkinsonism, and tardive dyskinesia (TD), which affect patients' mood, cognition, appearance, and self-image. The neuroleptic syndrome (pejoratively referred to as the *zombie syndrome*) in the acute phases of schizophrenia and the disfiguring choreiform orofacial, peripheral, and truncal movements of TD in the chronic maintenance phase of the illness were powerful disincentives for patients with schizophrenia to adhere to treatment with first-generation antipsychotics, even when they experienced significant recovery from psychotic symptoms and were discharged from locked hospital wards to the community. Relapse secondary to noncompliance was the main reason for the 'revolving door' phenomenon, with patients predictably rehospitalized a few weeks or months after discharge. The frequent readmissions made schizophrenia a costly disease to society (estimated at about $65 billion annually) and prevented patients' full recovery and reintegration into the mainstream of society. Patients with schizophrenia, their long-suffering families, and the public at large developed a sense of hopelessness and a stigma about schizophrenia because of its chronicity, recurrence, and downward functional spiral socially and vocationally.

Another consequence of the limited efficacy and intolerable side effects of first-generation antipsychotics is the lifetime suicide rate of 10% in patients with schizophrenia, which is about 10 times higher than the rate in the general population. As will be discussed in the next chapter, the advent of the second-generation antipsychotics, labeled 'atypical' because of the minimal EPS associated with them, represents a major advance in the pharmacologic treatment of schizophrenia and other psychoses. The importance of avoiding EPS with antipsychotic treatment cannot be overemphasized because of the multiple negative consequences that EPS impose on patients with schizophrenia, who must receive antipsychotic medication for the rest of their life after their initial psychotic episode.

The side effects of first-generation antipsychotics can be broadly divided into two categories: central nervous system (CNS) effects and non-CNS effects (Table 7-4).

CNS Effects

The various CNS effects of the first-generation antipsychotics can be readily predicted from their neurotransmitter action profiles, which include one or more of the following: D_2 receptors, muscarinic cholinergic (M_1) receptors, α-adrenergic (α_1) receptors, and histamine (H_1) receptors. Low-, medium-, and high-potency neuroleptics have differential binding to these receptors and thus produce different side effects (Table 7-5).

Haloperidol is a prototype high-potency first-generation antipsychotic with low sedation (low H_1 receptor affinity), low anticholinergic effects (low M_1 receptor affinity), and low orthostasis (low α_1 receptor affinity) but high EPS (caused by potent D_2 receptor antagonism). At the other extreme, thioridazine (Mellaril®) is a prototype low-potency first-generation antipsychotic with an opposite profile: sedating, anticholinergic, and hypotensive but with mild EPS. Medium-potency first-generation antipsychotics such as perphenazine (Trilafon®) fall between haloperidol and thioridazine in their side-effect profile.

Sedation can be useful in the acute phase of psychosis, but most patients develop tolerance to sedation over time. Most patients are instructed by their physicians to take their medications at bedtime and exploit sedation effects to help them sleep. Orthostatic hypotension can be more serious, especially in the elderly, who should avoid the risk of falls and hip fractures. However, adequate hy-

Table 7-4: Side Effects of the First-Generation Antipsychotics

CNS Side Effects

Neurologic
- Acute movement disorders (eg, dystonia, akathisia, dyskinesia, akinesia)
- Delayed-onset movement disorders (eg, tardive dyskinesia, tardive dystonia)

Cognitive
- Confusion
- Sedation
- Delirium
- Memory impairment
- Apathy

Other
- Lowered seizure threshold
- Neuroleptic malignant syndrome (NMS)
- Neuroendocrine effects
  - hyperprolactinemia
  - polyuria/polydipsia (SIADH)
- Poikilothermy (hypothermia or hyperthermia)

Peripheral Side Effects

Cardiovascular
- Orthostatic hypotension
- Reflex tachycardia
- Cardiac rhythm disturbances (eg, Q-Tc prolongation, T-wave blunting, PR prolongation, ST segment depression, heart block, torsades de pointes, ventricular tachycardia)

dration, bedtime medication, and instruction to not get out of bed or a chair too quickly can help avoid orthostatic hypotension in most patients. Anticholinergic

Peripheral Side Effects *(continued)*
  GI/Hepatic
- Dry mouth
- Nausea/vomiting
- Constipation
- Paralytic ileus
- Cholestatic jaundice

Metabolic
- Weight gain
- Hyperglycemia/diabetes
- Hyperlipidemia

Renal
- Urinary hesitancy
- Urinary retention
- Urinary tract infection

Sexual
- Menstrual irregularities
- Gynecomastia
- Galactorrhea
- Amenorrhea
- Impaired ovulation and spermatogenesis
- Erectile dysfunction
- Retrograde ejaculation
- Anorgasmia

(continued on next page)

effects are serious because of their adverse cognitive effects on memory and the subjective annoyance to patients (blurry vision, drug mouth, constipation, and

Table 7-4: Side Effects of the First-Generation Antipsychotics (*continued*)

Peripheral Side Effects (*continued*)
  Hematologic
  - Leukopenia
  - Agranulocytosis
  - Thrombocytopenic purpura
  - Hemolytic anemia
  - Pancytopenia

  Ocular
  - Blurred vision
  - Dry eyes
  - Narrow-angle glaucoma
  - Benign pigmentation
  - Lenticular opacities

  Cutaneous
  - Allergic rashes
  - Photosensitivity/skin burns
  - Decreased sweating

urinary retention), which impair the quality of life and increase noncompliance.

EPS, the most serious and intolerable side effects of the first-generation antipsychotics, include the following types of movement disorders, which tend to occur at various stages of the illness because of D_2 blockage in the nigrostriatal D_2 tract:

Dystonia: Dystonia is a sudden contraction of the muscles of the eyes, neck, limb, or trunk. This form of EPS usually occurs within the first few days of starting a first-generation antipsychotic. The patient can be quickly relieved by a parenteral injection of benzodiazepine, an anticholinergic drug (benztropine), or an antihistamine with strong anticholinergic action, such as diphenhydramine. The new antipsychotics rarely produce dystonic reactions.

Akathisia: Akathisia is a very uncomfortable sense of physical restlessness and inability to sit or stand without squirming or shifting one's feet. This 'physical anxiety' side effect can be very disturbing to patients and tends to occur in the first few weeks of treatment, usually in young adults. Anticholinergic drugs are not as efficacious in akathisia as in dystonia. Partial relief may be achieved with oral doses of the β-adrenergic blocker propranolol (Inderal®) or with a benzodiazepine such as lorazepam (Ativan®) or clonazepam (Klonopin®). Consideration should be given to decreasing the dose of the first-generation antipsychotic or switching to a low-potency first-generation antipsychotic. The new antipsychotics, which have become the first choice for antipsychotic treatment, are associated with very low rates of akathisia.

Bradykinesia and pseudoparkinsonism: After several weeks of first-generation antipsychotic treatment, many patients develop rigidity, bradykinesia, and drug-induced parkinsonism (especially older patients). Bradykinesia is often associated with bradyphrenia, a secondary cognitive slowing; dysphoria (secondary mood symptoms); and secondary negative symptoms that exacerbate the primary negative symptoms of schizophrenia (eg, flat facial expression, stiff posture, lack of speech). The general management approach was to give patients with pseudoparkinsonism one of the anticholinergic drugs (such as 2 to 6 mg/d of benztropine or 2 to 8 mg/d of trihexyphenidyl), also referred to as *antiparkinsonian drugs*, or the dopamine agonist amantadine (100 to 300 mg/d). However, a much more rational management would be to cut back the dose of the first-generation antipsychotic because pseudoparkinsonism represents a D_2 receptor occupancy greater than 78% to 80%. As mentioned earlier, studies by Kapur et al indicate that an occupancy of 65% of

Table 7-5: Comparison of the Side Effect Profiles of the First-Generation Antipsychotics

Drug	EPS (D_2 affinity)	Anticholinergic (M_2 affinity)
Low-potency phenothiazines (chlorpromazine, thioridazine)	Low	High
Medium-potency antipsychotics (perphenazine, loxapine)	Medium	Medium
High-potency antipsychotics (fluphenazine, haloperidol)	High	Low

D_2 receptors is probably sufficient to exert an antipsychotic effect. Unfortunately, in the past, clinicians interpreted the development of parkinsonism as an indication that an adequate antipsychotic dose had been achieved, and anticholinergic drugs were added (often prophylactically). Many patients with schizophrenia and elderly patients with dementia-related psychosis suffered physically, cognitively, and emotionally until the mechanism and rational management of parkinsonism caused by first-generation antipsychotics were understood. The new antipsychotics, at usual clinical doses, rarely produce parkinsonism as the first-generation antipsychotics do.

Tardive dyskinesia: This movement disorder usually occurs after prolonged exposure to first-generation antipsychotics and is characterized by abnormal, choreiform movements of one or more sets of muscles, most charac-

Orthostasis (α_1 affinity)	Sedation (H_1 affinity)	Weight Gain (H_1 affinity)
High	High	High
Medium	Medium	Medium
Low	Low	Low

teristically the tongue, jaw, perioral, and facial muscles. Some patients initially manifest TD with abnormal choreiform finger and hand movements, others with truncal or neck movements. The differential diagnosis is shown in Table 7-6. The movements can be stopped very briefly by the patient, become worse when the patient is anxious, subside completely during sleep, and can be disfiguring and embarrassing to patients and cause them to avoid socializing or appearing in public. TD is often, but not always, irreversible. Brain imaging studies have shown that the caudate nucleus is hypertrophic in TD (because of proliferation of D_2 receptors as a reaction to chronic blockage) and regresses in size when TD is successfully treated (such as with clozapine).

Prospective studies have established that TD annual incidence in young adults is 5% with the administration

Table 7-6: The Differential Diagnosis of Tardive Dyskinesia

- Naturally occurring choreiform movement disorder in never-medicated schizophrenia
- Genetic neurologic disorders
  - Huntington's disease
  - Wilson's disease
  - Basal ganglia calcification
  - Familial dystonias
- Acquired neurologic disorders
  - Postanoxic movement disorders
  - Postencephalitic movement disorders
  - Brain tumors
  - Age-related 'mouthing' (orobuccal movements)
- Drug-induced disorders
  - Stimulants
  - Levodopa and other dopamine agonists
  - Anticholinergics
  - Lithium
  - Anticonvulsants
  - Heavy metal poisoning

of first-generation antipsychotics and plateaus after 10 to 12 years at a total cumulative rate of 50% to 60%. On the other hand, geriatric patients exposed to first-generation antipsychotics develop TD at a much higher rate of 25% to 28% at the end of the first year, increasing to 50% after the second year of neuroleptic exposure. These studies underscore the importance of avoiding first-generation antipsychotics, especially in older patients. Studies with the new antipsychotics show a 10-fold decrease in annual TD rates in young and old patients (0.5% and 2.5% after 1 year, respectively).

TD should be distinguished from withdrawal dyskinesia when first-generation antipsychotics are abruptly stopped. Patients must be screened at least every 3 months for TD using the Abnormal Involuntary Movement Scale (AIMS). There are no known effective treatments for TD despite a large number of studies. Recent studies have shown that clozapine can reverse previously irreversible TD after 6 to 12 months. Studies with other atypical new antipsychotics are being conducted after several case reports of improvement of TD by those antipsychotics. Tardive akathisia, tardive dystonia, and tardive pain (orogenital) syndromes can occur with first-generation antipsychotics.

Other CNS effects of first-generation antipsychotics are hyperprolactinemia and the syndrome of inappropriate antidiuretic hormone (SIADH). Hyperprolactinemia results from D_2 receptor blockage in the hypothalamic D_2 tract, where prolactin is tonically inhibited by dopamine. All first-generation antipsychotics increase serum concentration of prolactin. Some patients with elevated prolactin experience sexual side effects such as reduced libido, enlarged breasts (gynecomastia), false breast milk (galactorrhea), infrequent menstruation (oligomenorrhea), or absent menstruation (amenorrhea). However, sexual dysfunction can be caused by other factors in schizophrenia such as heavy smoking (70% to 80% of patients with schizophrenia are heavy smokers), stress, hypothyroidism, diabetes, weight loss, and substance abuse. Prolonged amenorrhea may be associated with osteoporosis caused by hypoestrogenemia. If reducing the antipsychotic dose or adding a dopamine agonist (bromocriptine 0.5 mg/d) does not restore menstruation, a switch to another antipsychotic should be considered.

The mechanism of SIADH in schizophrenia is not well understood, but it tends to occur in chronic, treatment-resistant, or treatment-refractory patients. Medical management of water intake is necessary in such patients. The new antipsychotics have been noted to reverse SIADH in patients with chronic schizophrenia.

Seizures are an infrequent side effect of the first-generation antipsychotics. Low-potency phenothiazines tend to reduce the seizure threshold more than the other antipsychotics. Patients with a history of seizure disorder must be monitored more vigilantly if they receive a low-potency phenothiazine.

Thermoregulatory effects: Neuroleptic malignant syndrome (NMS) is known to occur with all first-generation antipsychotics and is reported with clozapine and other new antipsychotics. It is characterized by muscle rigidity, hyperthermia, autonomic instability, leukocytosis, fluctuating consciousness, and elevated creatine phosphokinase. NMS can be fatal in about 10% of cases (an incidence of 0.21% to 3% in various studies). Risk factors include rapid (especially parenteral) titration of antipsychotics, dehydration, preexisting neurologic or mood disorder, agitation, and concurrent use of lithium. Medical stabilization is important, including dantrolene, dopamine agonists, and even electroconvulsive therapy (ECT). Catatonia must be ruled out in the differential diagnosis of NMS patients.

Because of the poikilothermy associated with first-generation antipsychotics, patients can become hyperthermic or hypothermic, depending on the ambient temperature. Thus, patients receiving first-generation antipsychotics should not be exposed to temperature extremes.

Non-CNS Effects

There are several important medical side effects that can occur in the course of treatment with first-generation antipsychotics.

Cardiovascular effects: These include postural hypotension, which occurs mainly with the low-potency antipsychotics (aliphatic and piperidine phenothiazines). Tachycardia secondary to anticholinergic effects of the same low-potency first-generation antipsychotics is also seen in some patients. However, the most serious cardiovascular effects are related to cardiac rhythm disturbances such as

Q-Tc prolongation, T-wave blunting, PR prolongation, ST segment depression, heart block, torsades de pointes, ventricular tachycardia, and ventricular fibrillation or sudden death. Many of these cardiac rhythm disturbances are also seen with other psychotropic drugs, which is important because patients with schizophrenia sometimes receive other psychotropics that may have additive effects.

Of all the first-generation antipsychotics, thioridazine has been associated with the largest number of cardiac adverse events in the published literature. For example, it has the longest Q-Tc effect (31 msec) of any antipsychotic, old or new, and there are more reports of sudden death associated with it than with any other antipsychotic. On the other hand, haloperidol, which has a modest effect on the Q-Tc (10 msec) in the oral form, has been associated with several cases of torsades de pointes or death when used intravenously in intensive care units. Thus, all the first-generation antipsychotics must be used with great care in patients at risk for cardiac disease, especially those with rhythm disturbances. Except for clozapine, the new antipsychotics have rarely been associated with life-threatening cardiac side effects.

Hematologic effects: Some blood dyscrasias occur in conjunction with first-generation antipsychotics, mostly with the low-potency phenothiazines (about 0.32%). These include leukopenia, agranulocytosis, pancytopenic purpura, and thrombocytopenic purpura. Agranulocytosis (defined as a granulocyte count below $500/mm^3$) is the most serious of these hematologic effects and requires urgent medical care when it occurs.

Of the new antipsychotics, only clozapine has been associated with a risk of agranulocytosis (1% rate). None of the other new antipsychotics has been restricted with weekly white blood cell checks like clozapine, which is approved for use only in refractory schizophrenia.

Weight gain: The low-potency phenothiazines, especially thioridazine, are associated with the greatest degree

157

of short-term weight gain, while high-potency first-generation antipsychotics such as haloperidol or fluphenazine (Prolixin®) have a minimal effect on weight gain. Molindone (Moban®) is the first-generation antipsychotic that causes the least weight gain (it is essentially weight neutral). Most patients with chronic schizophrenia are overweight (body mass index of 25 to 30 kg/m^2) or obese (body mass index > 30 kg/m^2), regardless of which first-generation antipsychotic they receive. This reflects their poor nutritional habits and sedentary lifestyle during their chronic illness.

Glucose and lipid metabolism: Before the phenothiazine era, patients with schizophrenia (or bipolar disorder) were reported to be at twofold to threefold risk of diabetes even before receiving antipsychotics. However, the prevalence of diabetes in schizophrenia patients was noted to increase significantly after the introduction of chlorpromazine, a low-potency phenothiazine. In addition, thioridazine, which also causes significant weight gain, was observed to trigger new cases of diabetes in patients with schizophrenia. Most of these cases are late-onset, obesity-related type 2 diabetes. However, some of the new antipsychotics (especially clozapine and olanzapine) have now been observed to be associated with not only noninsulin-dependent diabetes mellitus, but also diabetic ketoacidosis in the absence of significant weight gain, along with a significant increase in serum lipid levels, especially triglycerides. Metabolic disorders have emerged as the most serious adverse effects of some new antipsychotics (see Chapter 8).

Gastrointestinal/hepatic effects: First-generation antipsychotics have been associated with nausea and vomiting, as well as dry mouth, constipation, and even paralytic ileus, associated with the anticholinergic effects of low-potency phenothiazines. Liver effects include jaundice (increased bilirubin) and increased alkaline phosphatase. Some patients develop idiosyncratic hepatotoxicity with the phenothiazine class of first-generation antipsychotics.

Ocular effects: In addition to anticholinergic-related blurred vision, dry eyes, and acute narrow-angle glaucoma, first-generation antipsychotics (especially thioridazine, chlorpromazine, and thiothixene) produce benign, irreversible retinal pigmentation. However, recent studies indicate that in addition to retinal pigmentation, a substantial proportion of patients with chronic schizophrenia have lenticular opacities. Two studies in young patients (in their 30s) receiving first-generation antipsychotics show a 22% to 26% prevalence of cataracts compared with a general population rate of 0.2%. This 100-fold increase in cataracts may be related to other risk factors for cataracts present in patients with schizophrenia, such as ultraviolet ray exposure, heavy smoking, diabetes, stress, and facial trauma. The study authors were so surprised by the high cataract rate that they suggested that abnormal pathophysiology of schizophrenia may predispose patients to lenticular opacities as a comorbidity.

Cutaneous effects: The first-generation antipsychotics often cause photosensitivity reactions (excessive sunburn even with brief exposure to the sun) and allergic rashes.

First-Generation Antipsychotics and Special Populations

Pregnant Patients

There is extensive literature about the use of older antipsychotics (especially chlorpromazine and haloperidol) in pregnant patients as antiemetics in pregnancy-induced nausea/vomiting and for managing psychotic symptoms. The consensus is that there is no evidence of significantly increased congenital anomalies from the use of the first-generation antipsychotics or the anticholinergic medications that were frequently given with them. These drugs are all rated by the FDA as category C. However, the literature on behavioral teratogenicity is not conclusive, and the confounding factor of breast-feeding and the additional exposure of infants to antipsychotics in breast milk should also be taken into account.

The consensus of researchers and clinicians has been that not treating psychosis during pregnancy is far riskier to mother and fetus than the potential teratogenic effects of antipsychotics.

Ethnic Populations

There is growing evidence that different ethnic populations may vary genetically in their metabolism of various drugs such as the old and new antipsychotics. Ethnic differences in the cytochrome P450 enzyme system are now well established, particularly in CYP2D6, CYP3A4, and CYP1A2, which collectively oxidize most psychotropic drugs, including first-generation antipsychotics. Individuals may be ultrarapid metabolizers, extensive metabolizers, or slow metabolizers, depending on the multiple allelic variants of a cytochrome enzyme, referred to as *polymorphism*. For example, there is a high prevalence of slow metabolism of drugs that are metabolized by CYP2D6 in African and Asian populations because these populations tend to have a certain genetic variant of this enzyme. The implication of these ethnic metabolic differences is that while a white patient may tolerate a dose of 5 mg of haloperidol per day, the same dose may produce serious neurologic side effects in a patient of African or Asian descent who may be a slow metabolizer and would thus have a slow clearance of the drug. Thus, EPS and TD have been noted to be higher in African-American patients because most practitioners medicate them with the same dose as white patients.

Heavy Smokers

Many patients with schizophrenia (70% to 80%) are heavy smokers. Because tobacco induces cytochrome enzymes (such as CYP1A2), smoking may significantly increase the oxidation of some antipsychotics, essentially reducing the serum concentrations and bioavailability of the antipsychotic. When combined with poor compliance, this may predispose patients to relapse unless higher doses are given. It has long been believed that heavy smoking provided relief from EPS in some patients by titrating down the dose of the antipsychotic. This should be taken into account when a patient receiving antipsychotics is encouraged to quit smoking, which will result in more potential side effects because of a decrease in the clearance of the antipsychotic and a rise in the serum concentrations.

Mental Retardation

Many developmentally disabled patients, often children and adolescents, manifest severe agitation and/or bizarre behavior that prompts treatment with antipsychotics. Diagnosis can be difficult in uncommunicative patients with aggression, panic attacks, agitated depression, or aggression psychosis—all manifesting with a similar clinical presentation. First-generation antipsychotics were used extensively and usually in high doses to manage the behavioral problems of mentally retarded or mentally ill patients, who tend to have disproportionately high rates of EPS and TD. Preexisting brain pathology tends to predispose such patients to iatrogenic movement disorders. As will be discussed in the next chapter, the new antipsychotics are safer and preferred for the treatment of this population.

Noncompliant Patients

Studies indicate that after discharge from inpatient treatment, 24% to 88% of patients with schizophrenia will do one of the following: (a) refuse to take their maintenance medications (some may not even accept or recognize that they are ill, because loss of insight is common in schizophrenia), (b) stop taking their medications because of intolerable side effects such as EPS, or (c) take part of the dose or skip some doses entirely because of cognitive deficits or lack of a caregiver to monitor their compliance. The high rates of noncompliance, partial compliance, or dyscompliance account for a significant proportion of the high relapse rate in patients with chronic schizophrenia. Physicians often try to simplify the dose schedule to a once-daily dose to facilitate compliance, but some patients still fail to take their maintenance dose regularly.

Long-acting depot formulations are available for fluphenazine and haloperidol, both of which have a hydroxyl moiety that allows them to be esterified and put in an oily base for slow-release depot injection every 2 to 4 weeks. These first-generation antipsychotic depot regimens are given to about 10% of patients with chronic schizophrenia in community mental health centers, Veterans Affairs medical centers, or university-based outpatient clinics, where many patients with schizophrenia receive their psychiatric care. Clinically, perhaps up to 40% of patients with chronic schizophrenia would benefit substantially from depot antipsychotic parenteral injections every 2 to 4 weeks to help reduce their high relapse rate. However, because of their side effects, especially acute EPS (primarily akathisia) or long-term TD, depot first-generation antipsychotics are restricted to use in only the sickest and most cognitively or socially disorganized patients. The advent of long-acting preparations of atypical new antipsychotics (the first to be launched is Risperdal Consta®) will enable clinicians to use parenteral biweekly injections in a larger proportion of patients with schizophrenia. This management is addressed further in the next chapter. Sustained compliance (medication taking) and adherence (keeping appointments and following the physician's overall treatment plan) are important to recovery, long-term restoration of functioning, and quality of life in schizophrenia.

Treatment Resistance and Refractoriness

One of the major challenges in the pharmacotherapy of schizophrenia with first-generation antipsychotics is the development of some degree of treatment resistance (Table 7-7) in up to 50% of patients within 2 to 5 years of the onset of psychosis (usually the same time as first hospitalization). A subset of patients with schizophrenia (about 25% of all patients) is considered treatment refractory. The definition of treatment resistance is the persistence of psychotic (positive) symptoms at a lower intensity than

Table 7-7: Degrees of Schizophrenia Treatment Resistance to the First-Generation Antipsychotics

• **Treatment refractoriness:** Two or more adequate antipsychotic drug trials (at least 6 weeks' duration and a dose of at least 400 to 600 mg chlorpromazine equivalents daily) with no clinical improvement in the positive symptoms

• **Treatment resistance:** Persistence of the positive symptoms at a level exceeding a total score of 45 on the Brief Psychiatric Rating Scale (BPRS)

• **Persistence of illness:** Continuous period of 5 years or more with poor social or occupational functioning (often caused by severe negative and cognitive impairment)

in the acute stage. Treatment refractoriness is defined as the almost complete lack of response of the psychotic symptoms to two to three adequate trials of antipsychotic therapy. Researchers define refractoriness as having a BPRS (Brief Psychiatric Rating Scale) score of greater than 45 and absence of a stable period of social or vocational functioning in the last 5 years (Table 7-7).

The reasons why patients develop treatment resistance in schizophrenia are not yet established. Lieberman and colleagues found that in contrast to first-episode patients with schizophrenia, 90% of whom respond well after 8 to 52 weeks of treatment, the response rate is much lower (48%) when the same antipsychotic treatment is given to patients who have had several episodes of illness. It should also be noted that in the era of the first-generation antipsychotics (1950s to 1980s), treatment response in schizophrenia referred to the suppression of positive symptoms (predominantly delusions and hallucinations) and not to the entire spectrum of psychopathology in schizophrenia, including negative deficit symptoms, cognitive dysfunction, and mood-anxiety symptoms. First-generation antipsychotics have minimal efficacy on the latter symptom domains, leaving most patients chronically impaired because of social withdrawal; lack of drive; impoverished thinking; blunted affect; attention deficit; impaired memory, learning, and executive functions; depression; anxiety; and frequent substance abuse. If all symptom domains are considered, most patients with schizophrenia are treatment resistant to first-generation antipsychotics.

Supplemental Treatments in Schizophrenia

Until the approval of clozapine in the United States for treatment-refractory schizophrenia, around 1990, patients who failed to respond to first-generation antipsychotics could not be discharged and were kept in institutional settings for many years. Researchers examined the efficacy of adding several other psychotropic medications or somatic treatments in treatment-resistant patients, with mixed success. The following are some of the non-neuroleptic treatments that were used as adjunctive therapies (Table 7-8) for treatment-resistant or treatment-refractory schizophrenia in the era of first-generation antipsychotics.

Benzodiazepines

Most often, benzodiazepines were added to first-generation antipsychotic therapy to help in managing anxiety, agitation, or movement disorders (eg, akathisia, dystonia, catatonia). An extensive review of the literature indicates that benzodiazepines did help reduce such symptoms in patients with chronic schizophrenia, although they did not help the psychotic symptoms. Short-acting benzodiazepines, such as lorazepam, are still commonly used orally or parenterally in emergency room settings along with an oral antipsychotic to calm agitated or aggressive patients and as medications in inpatient settings when patients' agitation symptoms

> **Table 7-8: Drugs That Have Been Used to Augment the First-Generation Antipsychotics in Schizophrenia (For Positive, Negative, and Mood Symptoms)**
>
> - Benzodiazepines (diazepam, lorazepam)
> - Mood stabilizers (lithium, valproate, carbamazepine)
> - Antidepressants (tricyclics, selective serotonin reuptake inhibitors)
> - β-blockers (propranolol)
> - Dopamine agonists (amphetamine, levodopa)
> - NMDA agonists (glycine)
> - Monoamine depleters (reserpine)

occasionally worsen. It is generally believed that gamma-aminobutyric acid drugs may help dopamine receptor antagonists (ie, first-generation antipsychotics) in managing the spectrum of behavioral and anxiety symptoms in schizophrenia. It should also be noted that megadoses of the benzodiazepine diazepam (up to 400 mg/d) have been reported to suppress psychotic symptoms (delusions and hallucinations) in controlled trials. However, the use of such large doses of benzodiazepines has never been adopted in clinical practice, even for the management of treatment-resistant or treatment-refractory schizophrenia.

Lithium

This mood stabilizer, known to be effective in bipolar disorder, has limited efficacy as a monotherapy for psychosis and may even worsen symptoms in some patients. However, several studies indicate that using lithium as an adjunctive medication with antipsychotics may enhance the management of treatment-resistant schizophrenia. The efficacy of adjunctive lithium is especially noted for comorbid affective symptoms such as irritability, impulsivity, and violent behavior, which are often seen in severe mania. The main drawbacks to using lithium are its potential neurotoxic side effects when combined with the first-generation antipsychotics, including memory dysfunction and tremor, as well as gastrointestinal side effects.

Anticonvulsants

Some studies have found that mood anticonvulsants, especially valproate (Depakote®), may augment the efficacy of first-generation antipsychotics, especially for manic symptoms. Another use for adjunctive anticonvulsants is to protect patients from a concurrent seizure disorder or from the lowering of the seizure threshold by the older antipsychotics (especially chlorpromazine and thioridazine) or even by some new antipsychotics such as clozapine. A recent controlled study showed that the onset of antipsychotic action of risperidone and olanzapine is significantly faster when divalproex sodium is added at doses of up to 2,000 mg/d and a serum concentration of about 80 to 100 µg/dL.

Antidepressants

Because depression is a common comorbidity in schizophrenia (up to 60%), antidepressant drugs were often added to a regimen of first-generation antipsychotics for depressed patients with schizophrenia or schizoaffective disorder. The tricyclic antidepressants that were widely used in the 1970s and 1980s were largely replaced by selective serotonin reuptake inhibitors (SSRIs) in the 1990s. In addition to helping with depression, SSRIs, known for their broader actions, improve anxiety, obsessive-compulsive, and posttraumatic stress disorder symptoms, all of which are known to coexist with schizophrenia, especially the treatment-resistant subtype. However, while SSRI augmentation of older antipsychotics has been beneficial, there are potential pharmacokinetic interactions that can pose risks. Specifically, fluoxetine (Prozac®) and paroxetine (Paxil®)

are potent inhibitors of cytochrome P4502D6 and reduce metabolic clearance of many antipsychotics, causing subsequent side effects or toxicity. Similarly, fluvoxamine (Luvox®) is an inhibitor of the CYP1A2 enzyme and could cause toxicity if used with clozapine or olanzapine. The safest SSRIs to use as adjuncts with antipsychotics are sertraline (Zoloft®) and citalopram (Celexa™) because of their lack of kinetic interactions.

β-*Blockers*

At small doses, β-blockers are known to reduce antipsychotic-induced akathisia and related somatic anxiety symptoms. Some studies using megadoses (up to 1,200 mg of propranolol) have reported an augmentation of first-generation antipsychotics for treatment-refractory positive symptoms. However, those high doses are rarely used, especially since a new generation of antipsychotic drugs is now available.

Somatic Therapies

Unusually drastic measures, including frontal lobotomy and insulin coma, were used before the introduction of the first-generation antipsychotic drugs to control aggressive psychotic symptoms. While such controversial interventions were discontinued after the availability of pharmacotherapy for psychosis, the management of treatment-refractory schizophrenia, especially in the 1960s and 1970s, prompted the use of ECT, a somatic treatment with established efficacy in severe mood disorder. Several studies, mostly uncontrolled, have shown that ECT may help an occasional patient, but it does not seem to be useful as a routine add-on to patients with resistance or refractoriness to first-generation antipsychotics. Patients with schizophrenia most likely to benefit from ECT are those with catatonia or severe depression. Technological advances (pulse wave instead of sine wave) and the use of unilateral nondominant hemisphere ECT appear to minimize cognitive sequelae of ECT when used for psychiatric treatment.

Conclusions

The first generation of antipsychotics, now referred to as *conventional antipsychotics*, represented a major breakthrough in the treatment of schizophrenia and other psychoses. However, they are being rapidly replaced by the second-generation antipsychotics (see Chapter 8) because their extensive use over 4 decades has established them as having limited efficacy as well as serious, often intolerable, side effects that reduce treatment adherence. The risk of acute EPS and irreversible neurologic consequences, such as TD, has been a major limitation in using the first-generation antipsychotics, but their lack of efficacy on negative, cognitive, mood/anxiety, and substance abuse comorbidities has been their major drawback in treating schizophrenia. Despite the suppression of delusions and hallucinations, few patients with schizophrenia regained their health and wellness with use of first-generation antipsychotics, and most patients suffered from poor quality of life and inability to regain their social and occupational functioning. It is not surprising that the new generation of antipsychotics, with broader efficacy on the symptom domains of schizophrenia and minimal EPS, has supplanted the older antipsychotics and promises to raise the standard of care in psychosis management. Also gratifying is the usefulness of the new antipsychotics in many nonpsychotic disorders that the first-generation antipsychotics did not help.

Suggested Readings

American Psychiatric Association: *Tardive Dyskinesia.* Washington, DC, American Psychiatric Press, 1999.

Arana GW, Hyman SE, Rosenbaum JF: *Handbook of Psychiatric Drug Therapy.* New York, Lippincott, Williams and Wilkins, 2000.

Bezchlibnyk-Butler KZ, Jeffries JJ, eds. *Clinical Handbook of Psychotropic Drugs.* Toronto, Hogrefe and Huber Publishers, 2000.

Frances A, Docherty JP, Kahn DA, eds. The Expert Consensus Guideline Series: treatment of schizophrenia. *J Clin Psychiatry* 1996;57(suppl 12B):11-58.

Kupfer DJ, Bloom FE, eds. *Psychopharmacology: The Fourth Generation of Progress.* New York, Lippincott-Raven, 1995.

Lieberman JA, Murray RM: *Comprehensive Care of Schizophrenia: A Textbook of Clinical Management.* London, Martin Dunitz Ltd, 2000.

Schatzberg AF, Nemeroff CB, eds. *The American Psychiatric Press Textbook of Psychopharmacology,* 4th ed. Washington, DC, American Psychiatric Press, 1995.

Shriqui CL, Nasrallah HA, eds. *Contemporary Issues in the Treatment of Schizophrenia.* Washington, DC, American Psychiatric Press, 1995.

Stahl SM: *Psychopharmacology of Antipsychotics.* London, Martin Dunitz Ltd, 1999.

Chapter **8**

The New Generation of Atypical Antipsychotics

After 4 decades (1950s to 1990s) of using the first-generation conventional antipsychotics, with their limited efficacy (on positive symptoms only) and intolerable side effects (particularly extrapyramidal side effects [EPS] and tardive dyskinesia [TD]), the need for a better class of antipsychotics was evident. Patients with schizophrenia were able to leave institutional settings when their delusions, hallucinations, and agitation subsided with the use of older antipsychotics such as haloperidol (Haldol®). However, most patients with chronic schizophrenia did not regain social or vocational functioning and often continued to manifest serious deficits (negative symptoms and cognitive impairments) that interfered with or complicated rehabilitation efforts. Furthermore, the lifetime suicide rate in patients with chronic schizophrenia remained very high (10%), reflecting the lack of efficacy of the older antipsychotics on comorbid depression, which afflicts up to 60% of patients with schizophrenia. These patients often become even more dysphoric with the older antipsychotics. Finally, the failure of the older antipsychotics to have any efficacy for about 25% of patients with 'refractory' schizophrenia required long-term inpatient institutionalization because of unabated psychosis and patients' inability to care for themselves or live independently outside institutional settings.

The evolution of the new generation of atypical antipsychotics occurred against a backdrop of disenchantment,

TD, widespread noncompliance, and a sense of frustration and hopelessness in patients, families, and physicians. The stigma of schizophrenia was exacerbated by the failure of the older antipsychotics to restore wellness and functioning and by the 'zombie' appearance of patients suffering from EPS and the associated neuroleptic syndrome.

Clozapine

The serendipitous discovery of clozapine (Clozaril®) in 1959 was the beginning of the atypical antipsychotic era. Compared to the numerous phenothiazines that were synthesized in the 1950s to create variations of the chlorpromazine (Thorazine®) structure, clozapine was a dibenzodiazepine with an unusual profile for an antipsychotic: it had no EPS. The clinical dogma among psychiatrists at that time was that EPS were necessary to ensure that antipsychotic efficacy was occurring, a notion that clozapine completely refuted. Although controlled trials proving clozapine's antipsychotic efficacy were completed in 1965, it was not launched in Europe until 1972, mainly because of the doubts surrounding the 'atypical' absence of EPS. Clozapine was not introduced in the United States because of concerns about its hypotensive effects and risks of seizures at higher doses. Only 3 years after its European launch, a report of several cases of agranulocytosis and death was followed by other reports, ultimately leading to the complete withdrawal of clozapine.

Clozapine was resurrected in 1988 with the publication of results of the mid-1980s landmark controlled trial demonstrating the clear superiority of clozapine over first-generation antipsychotics in the most severely ill patients with refractory schizophrenia. Clozapine was approved by the US Food and Drug Administration (FDA) for refractory schizophrenia only, and strict weekly monitoring of white blood cell count was required to detect agranulocytosis, which occurred in up to 1% of the patients receiving clozapine. Therefore, it was not the remarkable

Table 8-1: Classes of the Approved Second-Generation (Atypical) Antipsychotics (Serotonin-Dopamine Antagonists)

Class	Representative Drug (Generic and Trade Names)	Date of Launch (in United States)
Dibenzodiazepine	clozapine (Clozaril®)	1989
Benzisoxazole	risperidone (Risperdal®)	1994
Thienobenzodiazepine	olanzapine (Zyprexa®)	1996
Dibenzothiazepine	quetiapine (Seroquel®)	1997
Benzothiazolyl-piperazine	ziprasidone (Geodon®)	2001

absence of EPS (atypicality) that prompted the comeback of clozapine but its unique efficacy on both positive and negative symptoms in the most difficult subgroup of patients with schizophrenia, those who were refractory to several trials of the older antipsychotics.

The Paradigm of Atypicality

The introduction of the second-generation antipsychotics (Table 8-1) was possible because of a new paradigm in drug development based on clozapine's neurotransmitter affinities—stronger serotonin antagonism than dopamine D_2 receptor blockade. The new atypicals are generally more selective in their D_2 receptor blockade, targeting the mesolimbic and mesocortical dopamine tracts (the putative psychosis areas) and avoiding the nigrostriatal and tuberoinfundibular/hypothalamic tracts (where excessive D_2 blockade produces EPS and hyperprolactinemia, respectively). Thus, the currently available atypical antipsychotics—clozapine (Clozaril®), risperidone (Risperdal®), olanzapine (Zyprexa®), quetiapine (Seroquel®), and ziprasidone (Geodon®)—are also called *serotonin-dopamine antagonists*. A soon-to-be-launched new antipsychotic, aripiprazole (Abilitat®), uses a different mechanism: partial dopamine and serotonin agonist effects.

A new model for the neurobiological mechanism for atypicality was recently proposed by Kapur and Seeman based on dopamine receptor occupancy studies with various antipsychotics. They postulate that rapid dissociation of an antipsychotic from the dopamine D_2 receptor in the striatum (ie, transient occupancy) accounts for the minimal EPS. They do not see a role for serotonin receptor antagonism in atypicality, which had been proposed by Meltzer. Atypical antipsychotics vary in their affinity for D_2 receptors. Clozapine and quetiapine have the fastest dissociation (as measured by the K_{off}) from dopamine receptors, which explains their lack of EPS even at high doses.

Atypical antipsychotics differ significantly in their structure and in their profile of neurotransmitter affinities (Table 8-2). Thus, unlike the first-generation antipsychotics, which were considered interchangeable in the treatment of schizophrenia, the new atypicals may act differently in different patients, although, overall, they appear to be individually effective in about two thirds of patients. These differences offer potential advantages in treating a heterogeneous disorder like schizophrenia and appear to decrease the proportion of treatment-resistant and treatment-refractory patients.

Efficacy of the New vs the Older Antipsychotics

Controlled clinical trials (double-blind, placebo-controlled comparisons) that prompted the FDA to approve the four atypical antipsychotics now available in the United States demonstrate the following important clinical findings:

Table 8-2: Neurotransmitter Receptor Affinities of the Second-Generation (Atypical) Antipsychotics

	D_2	5-HT_{2A}	5-HT_{2C}
clozapine	+	++++	+
risperidone	++++	+++++	++++
olanzapine	++	++++	++++
quetiapine	+	++	−
ziprasidone	+++	+++++	+++++

+++++ = very high; ++++ = high;
+++ = moderately high; ++ = moderate;
+ = low; − = minimal

- Atypicals are superior to placebo for both positive and negative symptoms.
- Atypicals are at least as effective as older antipsychotics on positive symptoms and, in some cases (risperidone), are statistically superior to haloperidol.
- Atypicals exert a significant effect on negative symptoms compared to high-dose haloperidol (20 mg/d).
- All atypicals exert an antidepressant effect compared to placebo or haloperidol.

The broader efficacy of atypical antipsychotics on positive, negative, and mood symptoms makes them more likely than the older antipsychotics to reverse the various symptom domains of schizophrenia. In addition, evidence that new antipsychotics may improve cognition deficits in schizophrenia (eg, memory, attention, executive functions) has emerged in postmarketing studies, fueling optimism for further improvement and successful rehabilitation in the long-term treatment of schizophrenia (discussed later in this chapter).

$5HT_{1A}$	$5\text{-}HT_{1D}$	α_1	M_1	H_1
++	−	++++	++++	++++
+	+	++++	−	++
−	+	++	++++	++++
+	−	++	++	++++
++++	++++	++	−	++

Head-to-Head Efficacy Comparisons Among Atypicals

Atypical antipsychotics have become widely accepted as the first-line treatment of schizophrenia. About 85% of oral antipsychotics now prescribed in the United States are atypicals, with risperidone and olanzapine each having about 30% market share and quetiapine about 17%. With the imminent introduction of the first long-acting intramuscular atypical (risperidone, Risperdal Consta®), it is likely that most patients receiving depot haloperidol or depot fluphenazine (Prolixin®) (the only two long-acting older antipsychotics available in the United States) will be switched to the atypical formulation.

With this widespread use of atypicals as the first-line treatment of schizophrenia, studies of the comparative efficacy of atypicals are surprisingly few. There are two published double-blind, controlled studies of risperidone versus olanzapine, both sponsored by their respective pharmaceutical manufacturers. The study funded by olanzapine's manufacturer, Eli Lilly, Inc, concluded that olanzapine has a higher efficacy on negative symptoms and higher frequency of response of positive symptoms than risperidone. This study (Tran et al) was criticized for several serious methodological and statistical flaws. Another study with a similar design, sponsored by risperidone's manufacturer, Janssen Pharmaceutica, showed that risperidone and olanzapine have equal overall effects (as measured by the Positive and Negative Symptoms Scale, PANSS) but that risperidone has better efficacy on positive symptoms and mood/anxiety symptoms than olanzapine. This study avoided the methodological flaws of the Tran et al study.

A third study, not sponsored by either manufacturer, found that risperidone and olanzapine were equally effective in treating the acute psychotic phase after 4 weeks of hospitalization but that risperidone exerted better efficacy in the maintenance phase than olanzapine, as evidenced by significantly fewer positive symptoms at the end of 6 months in the risperidone group compared to the olanzapine group.

There are no other published controlled head-to-head studies of atypicals. A large, open-label study of quetiapine versus risperidone, sponsored by the manufacturer of quetiapine (AstraZeneca), showed equal efficacy on positive and negative symptoms for the two drugs but better efficacy on mood symptoms by quetiapine. A comparison of ziprasidone versus olanzapine by Pfizer showed equal clinical efficacy on positive, negative, mood, and cognitive symptoms, but significantly fewer metabolic side effects (weight gain, hyperglycemia, and hyperlipidemia) with ziprasidone.

Additional head-to-head data will become available because the manufacturers of soon-to-be-launched atypicals such as aripiprazole and iloperidone (Zomaril®) have conducted controlled comparisons versus risperidone and olanzapine as part of clinical drug-development trials preceding launch.

The manufacturer of ziprasidone (Pfizer Inc) conducted a controlled study of switching from haloperidol, olanzapine, and risperidone to ziprasidone. While the main purpose of the study was to compare gradual and abrupt switching, the outcomes indicate improvement in side effects rather than in efficacy with the switch to ziprasidone from all three drugs. Improvement in some cognitive tests was found after switching from haloperidol, risperidone, and olanzapine to ziprasidone. There is a growing literature that all atypicals improve cognition in schizophrenia but not necessarily the same cognitive domains (discussed later in this chapter).

The National Institute of Mental Health (NIMH) recently funded a large, multicenter, controlled study of the effectiveness (not just efficacy) of the four available first-line atypicals, clozapine, and one older antipsychotic (perphenazine [Trilafon®]). The study is known as CATIE (Comparative Antipsychotic Treatment Intervention Effectiveness). When completed, it will provide landmark data regarding the efficacy, safety, outcomes, and overall effectiveness among atypical antipsychotics and compare them to the medium-potency older antipsychotic perphenazine.

Until the CATIE data become available (circa 2004), the comparative efficacy of atypical antipsychotics will not be definitively known. However, a comparison of the 'effect size' of atypical antipsychotics in the published literature has provided insights into their relative efficacy on the total psychopathology of schizophrenia as reflected in the PANSS, which is the standard clinical rating scale of positive and negative symptoms in all the clinical trials. The range of improvement in the PANSS is almost identical for all four first-line atypicals: between 12 and 26 points over 6 weeks. This is true for risperidone (8 studies), olanzapine (4 studies), quetiapine (4 studies), and ziprasidone (3 studies). Thus, it appears that atypical antipsychotics are very similar in efficacy on positive and negative symptoms, although they may differ in degree

Table 8-3: Cognition in Schizophrenia: What Is Preserved and What Is Impaired

No Impairment	Mild Impairment
Word recognition	Perceptual skills
Long-term factual memory	Delayed recognition
	Confrontation naming

of efficacy on mood symptoms (depression, anxiety, hostility, aggression) or in pattern of cognitive improvements. However, atypical antipsychotics have well-established side-effect differences, which will be discussed below. Given the apparent similarity in efficacy, the overall effectiveness of the various atypicals may be linked to their medical adverse effects and tolerability.

Efficacy of Atypical Antipsychotics on Cognitive Deficits in Schizophrenia

Although cognitive deficits in schizophrenia have been widely studied and well established (Table 8-3), they were not given the same status and importance as positive and negative symptoms until recently. In fact, the advent of the new-generation antipsychotics has refocused the debate regarding the core pathology of schizophrenia. There is now growing support for the idea that cognitive impairment may represent the central deficit in a disease that has been widely regarded as a psychotic disorder. The functional disability associated with schizophrenia appears to be not so much from the positive or negative symp-

Moderate Impairment	Severe Impairment
Delayed recall	Serial learning
Distractibility	Executive functions
Immediate memory span	Vigilance
Visuomotor skills	Motor speed
Working memory	Verbal fluency

toms but from the multiple cognitive deficits of varying severity that have been detected in research rather than clinical settings. Some of the cognitive deficits are intertwined with negative symptoms.

Major reasons for the reemergence of cognition as a critical domain in the psychopathology of schizophrenia were the observations that:

- Even when the old generation of antipsychotics effectively controlled the positive symptoms of schizophrenia, the course of the illness was still a downward spiral to poor social and vocational functioning, indicating that other factors may determine the course of the illness (eg, cognitive impairments).
- The new-generation antipsychotics appear to repair, at least partially, the cognitive dysfunction in schizophrenia and to enhance clinical outcomes by improving such key brain functions as attention, memory, learning, and executive skills, in addition to improving positive, negative, and mood symptoms.

The discovery that the new atypical antipsychotics improve some of the cognitive dysfunction in schizophrenia was not part of the FDA registration trials (which focused primarily on positive and negative symptoms). It was in postmarketing research studies of clozapine (the first atypical, but approved only for refractory schizophrenia) and risperidone (the first atypical approved for first-line use in schizophrenia) that cognitive improvements were noted. Neurocognitive assessment of patients before and after treatment with the old as well as the new antipsychotics revealed that cognition was significantly improved by the new atypical antipsychotics compared to the old antipsychotics. Similar studies with the other new atypical antipsychotics (olanzapine, quetiapine, and ziprasidone) showed cognitive improvement with all of them compared to the old antipsychotics. Aripiprazole, which will be launched soon, also exerts significant cognitive improvements simultaneous with clinical efficacy on positive and negative symptoms.

Interestingly, the different atypical antipsychotics appear to have different effects on various cognitive domains in schizophrenia, which further confirms that they are different agents that are not interchangeable as the older-generation antipsychotics appeared to be.

For example, studies show that clozapine appears to improve attention, verbal fluency, and some executive functions, but not working, verbal, or spatial memory. Risperidone consistently improves working memory, executive functions, and attention, but less so verbal learning and verbal memory. Olanzapine improves verbal learning, verbal memory, verbal fluency, and executive function, but not attention, working memory, or visual learning and memory. Quetiapine's effects appear to be mainly on executive function, working memory, attention, and verbal fluency, and ziprasidone's cognitive effects appear to be on verbal learning, executive functions, and working memory. Studies comparing atypical antipsychotics in cognitive effects are therefore likely to show different effects depending on the cognitive areas treated. It is possible to imagine a treatment algorithm that uses the neurocognitive deficits profile of a given person with schizophrenia to guide the selection of the atypical antipsychotic to use first, or even the optimal combination of atypical antipsychotics (for which there are no controlled efficacy studies currently in the literature). Effective cognitive repair in patients with schizophrenia is important because the restoration of social/vocational functioning depends on it.

The new atypical antipsychotics also promise to greatly facilitate psychotherapeutic and rehabilitative treatment modalities in schizophrenia compared to the older antipsychotics. Intact attention, short-term memory, and the ability to learn new information or skills are all vital for effective psychotherapy, social skills training, or vocational rehabilitation. The lack of efficacy on cognitive functions by the older antipsychotics may explain the generally dismal outcomes in most patients with schizophrenia even when their psychotic symptoms remitted and they received psychosocial interventions. Studies of the synergy of atypical antipsychotics with psychosocial treatments are sorely needed.

Side Effects of Atypical Antipsychotics

As a class, the new atypical antipsychotics are significantly safer than the older antipsychotics with regard to neurological movement disorders. However, they can be associated with several adverse effects, some of which can be serious for long-term medical morbidity and mortality in persons who need to receive long-term antipsychotic therapy. The side-effect profiles of atypicals are more dissimilar than their efficacy profiles, which, as mentioned earlier, are quite similar at clinically equivalent doses. Thus, the side effects of atypical antipsychotics have become a rational basis for an algorithm of drug selection; that is, if the probability of good clinical response with any of the atypical antipsychotics is about 65% to 70% when used initially in an acute psychotic episode, then choosing an atypical that is most likely to be tolerated during the maintenance phase becomes the

Table 8-4: Medical Adverse Effects Associated With Atypical Antipsychotics

Neurologic
- Movement disorders
- Seizures

Metabolic
- Obesity
- Dyslipidemia
- Hyperglycemia/diabetes

Endocrine
- Diabetes
- Hyperprolactinemia

Cardiovascular
- Q-Tc prolongation
- Orthostatic hypotension

Other
- Hematologic
- Anticholinergic
- Sedation
- Ocular
- Hepatic

guiding principle of antipsychotic pharmacotherapy selection. Because patients with acute schizophrenia vary widely in their susceptibility to various side effects, customizing the algorithm of atypical antipsychotic selection will produce optimal outcomes. Drug tolerability has a direct impact on patient adherence, which in turn is a major factor in relapse prevention and successful outcomes.

The major side effects (outlined in Table 8-4) can be benign, serious, immediate, or long term, as discussed below.

Movement Disorders

The greatest safety advantage of the atypical antipsychotics is the low or minimal occurrence of acute or late-onset movement disorders, such as TD. The various types of EPS are discussed in Chapter 7. Iatrogenic movement disorders were the commonest and the most serious and intolerable side effects that undermined treatment adherence in many patients with schizophrenia who received those medications. The low incidence (or even lack) of EPS with the second-generation antipsychotics is the hallmark of their 'atypicality.' Avoiding EPS can also help avoid a cascade of secondary depression, negative symptoms, cognitive dysfunction, and other burdens that were commonly encountered in patients with schizophrenia treated with the older antipsychotics (Table 8-5).

Of the five atypical antipsychotics approved for use at this time, clozapine and quetiapine have essentially no EPS at any dose, allowing upward dose titration without concerns abut EPS. The other three atypical antipsychotics, risperidone, olanzapine, and ziprasidone, have minimal, if any, EPS at lower doses (1 to 3 mg/d of risperidone, 5 to 10 mg/d of olanzapine, and 40 to 100 mg/d of ziprasidone). However, the likelihood of EPS steadily increases at daily doses greater than 6 mg of risperidone, 15 mg of olanzapine, or 160 mg of ziprasidone. When an EPS does appear at higher doses of these three drugs, it is usually a mild form of akathisia or hypokinesia. Dystonia is rare.

There are several hypotheses as to why atypical antipsychotics produce low (or no) EPS. One is that they have selective affinity for dopamine D_3 and D_4 receptors in the mesolimbic and mesocortical brain regions (the putative psychosis areas) and not for the D_2 receptors in the striatum, the EPS region in the brain. Another explanation is that the potent serotonin 5-HT_2 receptor antagonism of the atypical antipsychotics helps reduce the likelihood of EPS by modulating dopamine release to avoid excessive hypodopaminergia, which leads to various EPS syn-

Table 8-5: The Burdens of EPS in Schizophrenia

Burden	Consequence
Neurologic Burden	
EPS: dystonia, akathisia, parkinsonism	Reduced quality of life
TD: irreversible motor movements	Neurotoxicity
Bradykinesia and bradyphrenia	Zombie syndrome
Management Burden	
Poor compliance/adherence	Frequent relapses
Polypharmacy	Additional side effects
Dopaminergic Deficit	
Dysphoria	Suicidality
Negative symptoms	Social stigma
Cognitive dysfunction	Functional impairment
Anhedonia	Lack of initiative
Anticholinergic Medications	
Memory deficit	Cognitive impairment
Blurry vision, dry mouth, constipation	Reduced quality of life and added costs

EPS = extrapyramidal side effects
TD = tardive dyskinesia

dromes. The third and most recent hypothesis is based on dopamine D_2 occupancy studies using positron emission tomography (PET) scans, done by Kapur and colleagues at the University of Toronto. Those studies found that a

Table 8-6: 1-Year Incidence of Tardive Dyskinesia with Atypical vs Conventional Antipsychotics

Population	Conventionals	Atypicals
Adult	5%	0.5%
Elderly	25%	2.5%

Kane 1995; Jeste et al 1995; Yeung et al 2001

D_2 occupancy of 65% is the threshold for antipsychotic response but that a D_2 occupancy of 78% to 80% is the biological threshold for EPS, regardless of whether old or new antipsychotics are used. The only exceptions, clozapine and quetiapine, which are clinically known to rarely produce EPS at any dose, seem to be incapable of a sustained D_2 occupancy of greater than 70% because of what appears to be an unusually transient or 'loose' affinity with rapid dissociation from the dopamine D_2 receptors. According to this model, even older antipsychotics with very strong D_2 binding and slow dissociation, such as haloperidol, can be given in intermittent doses (less frequently than daily) to achieve an optimal D_2 occupancy of greater than 65% but less than 78% to accomplish antipsychotic efficacy with no EPS.

One important corollary of these studies is that continuous D_2 blockade exceeding 65% is not necessary to control psychosis, as evidenced by the temporary (2 to 3 h) peak above 65% attained by daily doses of clozapine and quetiapine. The important implication of this model is that an adequate once-a-day dosage of any antipsychotic is sufficient to achieve and maintain antipsychotic efficacy regardless of the half-life of the antipsychotic drug. Thus, serum concentrations (pharmacokinetics) of antipsychotics may not be relevant for efficacy (pharmacodynamics). If confirmed by further studies, all antipsychotics can be given as a single daily dose (such as at bedtime), which is conducive to better medication compliance and overall treatment adherence and improved outcome.

The incidence of TD with the atypical antipsychotics has now been shown, in several studies, to be about 10-fold lower than that with the older antipsychotics. This is not surprising, given that acute EPS tend to predict TD occurrence in the long term. Annual TD rates with the old antipsychotics, consistently about 5% in young patients and 25% in geriatric patients, have dropped to 0.5% and 2.5%, respectively, with all the atypical antipsychotics (Table 8-6). It is possible to predict that TD will become an uncommon occurrence among persons with schizophrenia receiving atypical antipsychotics. Studies have also demonstrated that even irreversible TD secondary to older antipsychotics can be treated with clozapine and, possibly, other atypical antipsychotics.

Recent studies underscore the neurologic safety of atypical antipsychotics and the reason it is essential to use them as the first-line treatment of new-onset psychosis. Kopala and her collaborators in Nova Scotia found that 27% of carefully assessed first-episode, never-medicated patients with schizophrenia had evidence of EPS-like symptoms (eg, rigidity, hypokinesia). Even brief initial treatment with haloperidol, an older antipsychotic, increased the EPS prevalence to about 60%. After switching to atypical antipsychotics, the prevalence of EPS fell back to a minimum of 27%. On the other hand, when the older antipsychotics were avoided and atypicals were used as the initial treatment, the naturally occurring EPS prevalence fell from 27% to zero. Thus, it seems that exposing drug-naïve first-episode patients with schizophrenia to older antipsychotics may completely prevent the reversal of naturally occurring comorbid neuromotor disorder, which can be effectively normalized with atypical antipsychotics.

Table 8-7: The Serious Cascade of Adverse Health Effects of Weight Gain/Obesity

Short Term
- Fatigue
- Shortness of breath
- Sweating
- Back pain

Intermediate Term
- Arthritis
- Gall bladder disease
- Stress incontinence
- Snoring, sleep apnea, daytime sleepiness
- Low self-esteem/depression
- Hyperglycemia
- Hyperlipidemia

Long Term
- Hypertension
- Diabetes type 2
- Ischemic heart disease
- Stroke
- Cancer (breast, endometrial, colon, prostate)
- Premature death

As indicated earlier, clinicians should customize treatment to accommodate their patients' susceptibilities. There are certain patient populations that are at higher risk for EPS and that should be treated with the atypical associated with the lowest EPS, regardless of dose. Pivotal clinical trials and PET D_2 occupancy studies indicate that clozapine and quetiapine have minimal EPS regardless of dose. The populations at high risk for EPS include (1) the

Table 8-8: Weight Gain Profiles of Atypical Antipsychotics

	Mean Weight Gain (lb)	
	Short Term (8 weeks)	**Long Term**
High Weight Gain		
clozapine	9.5	29
olanzapine	9.2	26.5
Low Weight Gain		
quetiapine	4.6	4.8*
risperidone	4.5	4.7
Minimal Weight Gain		
ziprasidone	< 1	< 1

*A recent 1-year European study of monotherapy quetiapine found it to be weight neutral.

elderly, (2) first-episode psychosis patients, (3) patients with psychotic mood disorders, (4) children and adolescents, (5) mentally retarded/psychotic patients, (6) Parkinson's patients with levodopa psychosis, and (7) certain ethnic groups (Africans, Asians) with a high prevalence of slow metabolizers.

Weight Gain/Obesity Hyperlipidemia

Although weight gain and obesity are commonly associated with many of the older antipsychotics (especially low-potency phenothiazines), they were overshadowed by EPS and TD. With the significant decline in neurologic movement disorders with the atypical antipsychotics, weight gain and obesity have come to the forefront of serious adverse health effects of antipsychotic therapy. Like EPS, weight is associated with a cascade of health consequences culminating in serious medical morbidities and early mortality (Table 8-7).

The atypical antipsychotics can be categorized into three groups with regard to weight gain (Table 8-8). Olanzapine is associated with the greatest degree of mean weight gain (12.3 kg or 26.5 lb) after 1 year of use. This is similar to clozapine, the only atypical antipsychotic indicated for refractory schizophrenia. Quetiapine and risperidone are associated with a low mean weight gain (less than 5 lb) at the end of 1 year. It is not surprising that olanzapine and clozapine are also more associated with other metabolic disturbances in schizophrenia (hyperglycemia and hyperlipidemia) than the other atypical antipsychotics.

Scientific studies indicate that the threshold for health risk from weight gain is 7% above optimal body weight. This would be equivalent to a weight gain of 9 to 10 lb for an average woman and 14 to 15 lb for an average man. Thus, physicians must consider switching to another atypical if a patient reaches this risk threshold and should not wait until a weight gain of 15% to 20% occurs, as is often seen in clinical settings. However, it is very difficult to switch patients with refractory schizophrenia from clozapine if it is the only medication to which they respond. Reducing the dose of clozapine and combining it with an adjunctive dose of quetiapine, risperidone, or ziprasidone may be a practical option to help reduce serious weight gain with clozapine.

The causes of weight gain with atypical antipsychotics have not been fully elucidated. However, possible mechanisms include histamine H_1 affinity, serotonin 5-HT_{2c} pathways, satiety center dysfunction, slowed metabolism, and insulin resistance. Evidence exists that any combination of these factors may account for significant weight gain with atypical antipsychotics such as olanzapine and that some patients may be more susceptible than others to serious weight gain. Children and adolescents, women, first-episode psychosis patients, and patients with psychotic mood disorders appear to be particularly susceptible to significant weight gain with atypical antipsychotics. Thus, in customizing atypical antipsychotic therapy, olanzapine would not be the optimal first-line choice for these patients or for any patient who is explicitly opposed to gaining weight or who has a history of noncompliance when he or she starts gaining weight. Just as informed consent about the risks of EPS and TD was an integral step before prescribing first-generation antipsychotics, informed consent about serious weight gain and its related metabolic and health consequences may become necessary with atypical antipsychotics like olanzapine and clozapine.

Hyperlipidemia (especially hypertriglyceridemia), has been observed in patients receiving clozapine and olanzapine. Hyperlipidemia is a known correlate of obesity and increased body fat. However, some patients seem to develop hypertriglyceridemia disproportionate to a modest amount of weight gain, suggesting that other metabolic dysfunctions, such as insulin resistance (associated with an increased release of fatty acids into the circulation), may be an underlying mechanism. Again, atypical antipsychotics with the lowest weight gain effects should be considered for patients with high baseline serum lipids at baseline, and switches to other atypical antipsychotics should be implemented in patients who experience hyperlipidemia exceeding the normal range.

Diabetes

Late-onset (type 2) diabetes is a well-known consequence of obesity. Thus, it tends be a side effect of atypical antipsychotics that cause substantial weight gain, such as olanzapine and clozapine. However, the relationship between schizophrenia, diabetes, and antipsychotic therapy is complicated (Figure 8-1). Studies done in the 1940s and 1950s, before the discovery and use of the first-generation antipsychotics, indicated that patients with psychosis (schizophrenia and mania) had two to three times the rate of diabetes mellitus in the general population at

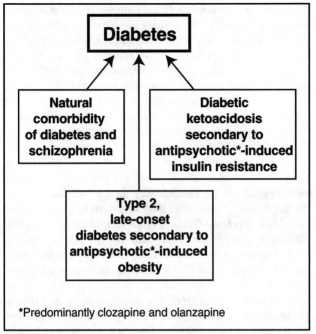

Figure 8-1: The pathways to diabetes in patients with schizophrenia.

that time (about 8% vs 3%). Thus, diabetes may be a medical comorbidity of schizophrenia, with possible genetic linkages that are yet to be determined. However, the naturally high diabetes rate in patients with schizophrenia doubled within a decade of the use of chlorpromazine, suggesting an additional, antipsychotic-induced increase in diabetes. Subsequent studies showed a similar increase in diabetes with thioridazine (Mellaril®), which is associated with the highest degree of weight gain among the older antipsychotics.

Among the atypical antipsychotics, more than 30 published reports have shown that clozapine and olanzapine are associated with a significant increase in diabetes (about 10% to 15%) after 1 to 2 years of use. A significant proportion of type 2 diabetes cases appear to emerge in patients who gain a substantial amount of weight with olanzapine or clozapine. However, several cases of a more serious form of acute diabetes (diabetic ketoacidosis) have also been reported, even in the absence of serious weight gain. Such cases require rapid management with insulin and, in some instances, admission to an intensive care unit because of the higher mortality risks.

Diabetes is not induced by clozapine and olanzapine simply via weight gain. Evidence is mounting that these two atypical antipsychotics may produce diabetes by inducing insulin resistance, which in turn can cause other metabolic adverse effects such as weight gain and hyperlipidemia. It is possible that patients with a family history of diabetes or a personal predisposition to diabetes may be at higher risk for developing insulin resistance with atypical antipsychotics. Many practitioners avoid using olanzapine as a first-line atypical antipsychotic in patients with a personal or family history of diabetes. However, for treatment-refractory patients in whom clozapine may be the only option, careful medical monitoring is necessary.

Management of new or exacerbated diabetes in patients receiving olanzapine includes a switch to risperidone, quetiapine, or ziprasidone, which have a much lower risk of diabetes. Insulin or oral hypoglycemic drugs may have to be used, but many patients may not need continued hypoglycemic therapy after several weeks of discontinuing olanzapine (or any other atypical antipsychotic) for the emergence of diabetes. Preventive measures include monitoring of fasting blood sugar (FBS) and hemoglobin A_{1c} at least every 3 months. A switch to another atypical antipsychotic must be considered if the patient's FBS exceeds 126 µg/dL, the definition of diabetes according to the American Diabetes Association.

Table 8-9: Potential Causes of Sexual Dysfunction in Schizophrenia

Condition	Potential Causes (besides hyperprolactinemia)
Amenorrhea or dysmenorrhea	Untreated schizophrenia
	Pregnancy
	Hypothyroidism
	Oral contraceptives
	Weight loss
	Obesity
	Stress
	Menopause
Decreased libido and erectile dysfunction	Untreated schizophrenia
	Smoking
	Substance abuse
	Diabetes
	Anxiety/depression
	SSRI treatment
Galactorrhea	Previous pregnancy
Decreased bone density	Smoking
	Sedentary lifestyle
	Poor nutrition
	Concomitant disease

SSRI = selective serotonin reuptake inhibitor

Hyperprolactinemia and Sexual Dysfunction

All the first-generation antipsychotics are associated with increased prolactin caused by dopamine antagonism in the tuberoinfundibular tract. Thus, a certain proportion of female patients develop amenorrhea, galactorrhea, gynecomastia, and decreased libido, and a certain proportion of male patients develop decreased libido and erectile dysfunction. Sexual dysfunction associated with hyperprolactinemia is an individual response; some patients have little dysfunction even at high prolactin levels, while others develop noticeable dysfunction with mild prolactin elevations.

Of the atypical antipsychotics, risperidone is associated with sustained hyperprolactinemia at practically any dose. Clozapine and quetiapine have a placebo-level profile of prolactin levels. Ziprasidone produces minimal hyperprolactinemia except at very high doses (greater than 200 mg/d), where a mild elevation occurs. Olanzapine produces only mild elevations at lower doses (5 to 10 mg/d) but significant elevations at high doses (30 to 40 mg/d).

Other factors may cause sexual dysfunction in schizophrenia (Table 8-9). Patients with sexual dysfunction that is clearly attributable to the antipsychotic should be switched to an antipsychotic with minimal prolactin increase, such as quetiapine or ziprasidone.

Q-Tc Prolongation

Many psychiatric and nonpsychiatric drugs can prolong the Q-T interval to varying degrees on the electrocardiogram (Table 8-10). The Q-Tc is the heart rate corrected Q-T interval. Most healthy individuals have a Q-Tc of about 400 ± 20 milliseconds (ms). However, Q-Tc is not a static parameter and can go up and down by as much as 70 ms on a given day because of any number of factors (Table 8-11). In general, the risk of torsades de pointes or ventricular fibrillation is generally believed to start above a Q-Tc of 500 ms.

Although many of the older antipsychotics caused significant Q-Tc prolongation, and despite the existence of

Table 8-10: Classes of Drugs Known to Prolong the Q-T Interval

- Antiarrhythmics
- Vasodilators/Anti-ischemics
- Anti-infectives
  - Antibiotics
  - Antimalarials
  - Antimycotics
- Antihistamines
- Psychotropics
  - Antidepressants
  - Antipsychotics

Table 8-11: Factors Associated With Transient Q-Tc Prolongation in Everyday Life*

- Eating
- Exercising
- Sleeping
- Obesity
- Taking medications
- Electrolyte imbalance (K+, Ca++, Mg++)
- Hypothyroidism
- Heavy alcohol use
- Cardiac disease
- Hypoglycemia

*In the range of 10 to 20 milliseconds

Table 8-12: Study 54: Metabolic Inhibitors

Study Drug	Metabolic Inhibitor
ziprasidone	ketoconazole
risperidone	paroxetine
olanzapine	fluvoxamine
quetiapine	ketoconazole
thioridazine	paroxetine
haloperidol	paroxetine ketoconazole

Pfizer Study 54: FDA Psychopharmacological Drug Advisory Committee, 2000

a large literature on sudden cardiac deaths among medicated patients with chronic schizophrenia, Q-Tc prolongation as a major potential adverse effect came to the forefront in conjunction with the launch of the most recent atypical antipsychotic, ziprasidone. This particular new antipsychotic, which was ready for launch in June 1998, was delayed by the FDA to conduct specific safety trials on Q-Tc. A rigorous, well-controlled study of ziprasidone as well as all the other first-line atypical antipsychotics that compared them to two first-generation antipsychotics (haloperidol and thioridazine) was conducted by ziprasidone's manufacturer, Pfizer. Q-Tc was measured before and after the addition of a metabolic inhibitor specific to each antipsychotic depending on which cytochrome enzyme oxidizes the antipsychotic (Table 8-12). The study was therefore designed to study the 'worst-case scenario' and to assess the effect of doubling or tripling the blood level of all atypical antipsychotics on the Q-Tc interval.

CYP Pathway/Inhibited	Study Days
CYP3A4	11-15
CYP2D6	19-25
CYP1A2	14-20
CYP3A4	13-17
CYP2D6	11-16
CYP2D6, CYP3A4	13-18

The study showed no increase in the Q-Tc by any of the atypical antipsychotics after metabolic inhibition. However, thioridazine was found to prolong the Q-Tc by 31 ms (and was subsequently given a black box warning by the FDA, which led to a drastic decline in its use in the United States). Ziprasidone did have a quantitatively (but not clinically significant) higher Q-Tc prolongation (17 ms) than haloperidol (11 ms), quetiapine (7 ms), risperidone (3 ms), and olanzapine (2 ms). There has been no evidence from almost 4,000 patients in clinical trials that ziprasidone is associated with torsades de pointes, even in 12 patients who took large overdoses of ziprasidone. After ziprasidone was approved by the FDA and launched in March 2001, more than 160,000 patients received it without cardiac safety problems, and the concern about the Q-Tc began to subside. Nevertheless, physicians should heed the warnings in the ziprasidone package insert regarding use of ziprasidone in patients who have cardiac disease or electrolyte imbalance or who are receiving other drugs with significant Q-Tc prolongation effects.

Ziprasidone is not metabolized exclusively via the 3A4 cytochrome; it has a major alternate aldehyde oxidase pathway that is not affected by induction or inhibition. This may explain why combining it with its metabolic inhibitor does not increase the Q-Tc risk.

Aripiprazole, an atypical antipsychotic to be released soon, was also found to have minimal Q-Tc effects. The FDA is now requiring Q-Tc safety studies to be conducted as part of the approval process of all new antipsychotic agents.

Orthostatic Hypotension

Postural hypotension is not a major problem with atypical antipsychotics, except for clozapine, especially in the early stages of treatment. A few patients (usually dehydrated and elderly) develop orthostasis with quetiapine, olanzapine, and risperidone. Nighttime dosing, proper hydration, and advice on not standing up too quickly can be helpful in most patients.

Sedation

Atypical antipsychotics vary in their sedative effects; clozapine, quetiapine, and olanzapine tend to cause greater levels of sedation. However, sedation is one side effect that may be useful in the acute psychotic phase and to which most patients develop tolerance over time.

Hematologic Effects

Clozapine is the only atypical antipsychotic with a serious potential for fatal agranulocytosis. Weekly leukocyte count has been highly effective in early agranulocytosis detection and clozapine discontinuation. Except for an occasional case in the literature, none of the other atypicals cause serious blood dyscrasias.

Anticholinergic Effects

The only atypical antipsychotics with clinically significant anticholinergic effects are clozapine and olanzapine, and more effects are reported with clozapine. Common patient complaints include blurry vision, dry mouth, constipation, and difficulty urinating. Acute angle-closure glaucoma has not been reported with atypical antipsychotics.

Ocular Effects

Many of the older antipsychotics are associated with ocular side effects such as lenticular opacities, pigmentation, or retinopathy. None of the atypical antipsychotics has been associated with adverse ocular effects in humans. Quetiapine was observed to produce species-specific cataracts in toxicology studies of beagle dogs receiving 400% of the therapeutic human dose. The package insert contains a precaution (not a warning), and eye examination is recommended (not mandated). A large follow-up study of more than 600,000 patients receiving quetiapine confirmed that it is not associated with cataracts in humans.

However, two recent studies done by ophthalmologists found that (1) more than 82% of young patients with schizophrenia have one or more ocular diseases and (2) about 24% of patients with schizophrenia have lenticular opacities (an astoundingly high rate exceeding 100 times the general population rate in young adults). These studies were done on patients who had not yet received any atypical antipsychotics and reflect the many cataract risk factors with which schizophrenia is associated, including smoking, diabetes, UV-ray exposure, stress, and trauma. Thus, a baseline examination for all patients with schizophrenia, regardless of the antipsychotic used, is good medical practice.

Seizures

Of the atypical antipsychotics, only clozapine is associated with a seizure risk, more so at higher doses (>600 mg/d). In patients with treatment-refractory schizophrenia who require high doses of clozapine or have a history of drug-induced seizures, the addition of valproate has been found to be useful.

Hepatic Effects

Olanzapine is sometimes associated with initial liver enzyme elevations that usually subside within 9 to 10 weeks. Patients with preexisting hepatic disease should be closely monitored.

Clinical Use of Atypical Antipsychotics

The atypical antipsychotics are now established as the first-line treatment for schizophrenia, and most evidence suggests that when they are used at the appropriate dose, they have similar efficacy in terms of the proportion of patients who improve significantly or in terms of the 'effect size' (ie, the quantitative decrease in psychopathology). After the failure of an adequate (10- to 14-week) trial of the first atypical antipsychotic, a similar monotherapy trial of a second atypical antipsychotic is indicated. Many clinicians exploit the 'add-then-taper' switching method to observe the effect of a temporary combination of atypical antipsychotics before going into monotherapy with the second drug. Opinions vary on performing a third monotherapy trial with yet another atypical versus going to clozapine with the assumption of treatment resistance after two failed atypical trials. It is reasonable to assume that physicians may use up to three different first-line atypical antipsychotics before opting to use clozapine, the best antipsychotic for refractory patients.

The clinical bottom line is, therefore, which atypical antipsychotic to select first and whether there is a rational and valid algorithm for the sequential use of atypical antipsychotics.

Surprisingly, there is no evidence-based guidance as to which atypical should be used first. The large, ongoing, NIMH-funded multicenter CATIE trial, comparing all four first-line atypical antipsychotics, clozapine, and the older antipsychotic perphenazine, may provide an answer to this question when data analysis of 1,800 subjects is initiated around 2004. Until then, the most reasonable clinical approach to selecting the first antipsychotic is based on the following: Since atypical antipsychotics appear to be similar in their overall efficacy in schizophrenia but different in their side-effect profiles, the selection of the first atypical antipsychotic for a given patient should be guided by and customized to that patient's biological susceptibility and tolerability to various medical adverse effects.

Thus, for patients susceptible to EPS (such as elderly, psychotic mood disorder, and first-episode psychosis patients and certain ethnic groups like African Americans), quetiapine, the atypical antipsychotic with placebo-level EPS, emerges as a rational first choice. In a patient highly sensitive to anticholinergic effects, risperidone, which has the fewest anticholinergic effects, is a good fit. Quetiapine or ziprasidone is an appropriate first choice for patients with a history of significant sexual dysfunction with older antipsychotics. For a patient with no family history of diabetes or hyperlipidemia but with cardiac conduction disease, olanzapine is a good choice. For a patient who is susceptible to weight gain or has high sensitivity to sedation, ziprasidone is an appropriate choice. For a patient with diabetes or hyperlipidemia or a first-degree family history of diabetes and hyperlipidemia, risperidone, ziprasidone, or quetiapine all make sense. The principle in these examples is that all four first-line atypical antipsychotics are useful, and it is fortunate that their profiles are diverse and can suit the needs of the heterogeneous populations suffering from schizophrenia (Table 8-13). New additions to the antipsychotic armamentarium, especially drugs with a novel mechanism of action (eg, aripiprazole), will provide more options for the treatment of schizophrenia and related psychoses. The long-acting intramuscular risperidone formulation that will be launched soon will also fill an urgent need for many patients with partial or poor compliance who relapse frequently and rarely achieve long-term clinical or psychosocial stability.

Although the atypical antipsychotics are approved mainly for schizophrenia, they are being regularly used for other psychotic disorders such as bipolar disorder and for a wide variety of axis I (eg, delirium, obsessive-compulsive disorder, anxiety, posttraumatic stress disorder), axis II (border-

Table 8-13: Practical Guideline for Selecting an Atypical Antipsychotic for Populations at Risk for Specific Side Effects

Side Effect	Populations at Risk
Extrapyramidal	Elderly; children; patients with first-episode psychosis, bipolar disorder, or levodopa-induced psychosis; certain ethnic groups (African Americans, Asians)
Prolactin-related sexual side effects	Adolescents and young adults
Weight gain	Children, adolescents, women, mood disorders, family history of obesity, diabetes, and hypertension
Diabetes	Overweight persons, personal or family history of diabetes
Hyperlipidemia	Overweight persons, personal or family history of hyperlipidemia or diabetes
Cardiac arrhythmia	History of chronic heart disease, family history of long Q-Tc, currently taking several drugs that prolong Q-Tc, low calcium or low magnesium

Optimal Atypical Antipsychotic(s)	Least Suitable Atypical Antipsychotic(s)
Quetiapine	High-dose risperidone (> 6 mg) Olanzapine (for levodopa psychosis in parkinsonism)
Quetiapine	Risperidone
Ziprasidone	Olanzapine
Quetiapine Risperidone Ziprasidone	Olanzapine
Risperidone Ziprasidone	Olanzapine
Olanzapine Quetiapine Risperidone	Ziprasidone

Table 8-14: Dosing of Atypical Antipsychotics in Schizophrenia

Antipsychotic	Initial Package Insert Instructions
risperidone (introduced 1994)	6 mg by the third day range 6-16 mg
olanzapine (introduced 1996)	10 mg/d range 10-20 mg
quetiapine (introduced 1997)	150-300 mg/d range 75-800 mg
ziprasidone (introduced 2001)	40-120 mg/d range 20-160 mg
clozapine (introduced 1974 and 1989)	400-600 range 100-1,000 mg

line, schizotypal, paranoid, and antisocial disorders), and axis III neurological disorders (eg, Tourette's syndrome, Parkinson's levodopa psychosis, Huntington's chorea). Research into the efficacy of atypical antipsychotics in nonpsychotic disorders will shed additional light on the neurobiology of both psychotic and nonpsychotic disorders and the overlapping pathophysiologies.

Dosing

The dosing patterns of atypical antipsychotics tend to change within a year or two of large-scale use in the 'real world.' Table 8-14 delineates differences from initial recommendations based on controlled clinical trials and the evolution of dosing in patients in various phases of schizophrenia. Risperidone was launched with aggressive dos-

| | Current Clinical Daily Dosing* | |
First Episode	Chronic/Relapsing	Treatment Resistant
2-4 mg	4-6 mg	6-8 mg
10-15 mg (higher doses for smokers)	15-30 mg	20-40 mg
400-600 mg	400-800 mg	600 + mg
40-120 mg	120-160 mg	160-200 mg
—	—	400-600 mg

*Based on practice patterns

ing recommendations (1 mg b.i.d. on day 1, 2 mg b.i.d. on day 2, and 3 mg b.i.d. on day 3, then going up to 16 mg/d if necessary). Within 2 to 3 years, most clinicians found lower doses to be effective and safe and began using smaller titration increments (with a national mean dose of 4.7 mg/d), rarely exceeding 6 mg because of the likelihood of EPS at higher doses. Further, q.d. dosing has replaced b.i.d. dosing as the standard maintenance regimen. With olanzapine, the opposite trend was the case: The initial dosing recommendations were too low (10 mg/d), and the mean dose grew steadily to about 18 mg/d, with some inpatients with acute psychosis requiring up to 40 mg/d. One of the factors for the escalating dose of olanzapine is that smoking (very prevalent in patients with schizophrenia) induces cytochrome 1A2 and accelerates the clearance of olanzapine, requiring higher doses. The initial prescribing message for quetiapine was confusing, suggesting efficacy at a wide range of 75 to 750 mg/d. Soon, practitioners found that doses lower than 300 mg/d had only partial efficacy in patients with schizophrenia and that 500 to 600 mg/d was the optimal dose range for these patients.

With ziprasidone, it is too early to predict, but the trend may be for a higher dose than that initially recommended (160 mg/d upper limit) for severe chronic schizophrenia. Clozapine is now being used at lower doses than were initially used in the late 1980s and early 1990s.

Finally, it should be noted that two intramuscular formulations of atypical antipsychotics for acute management of agitation during relapse in schizophrenia will soon be available. Both ziprasidone and olanzapine will become available in intramuscular formulation in 2002. Liquid formulation is available only for risperidone. A sublingual quick-dissolve formulation is available for olanzapine; one will soon be available for risperidone as well. Some atypicals (eg, quetiapine) are also being tested in sustained-release formulations.

Combination Therapy

It is estimated from pharmacy databases that about 25% of patients with schizophrenia in the United States are receiving combinations of antipsychotics, despite the lack of any controlled studies comparing monotherapy with combination therapy using atypical antipsychotics. Many physicians add atypical antipsychotics to a regimen of old antipsychotics when a patient (or family) refuses to change from the older antipsychotics. Another common combination is the addition of an atypical antipsychotic to a regimen of parenteral depot haloperidol or fluphenazine in noncompliant patients. The addition of an oral atypical antipsychotic is justified on the basis of trying to improve negative and mood symptoms as well as cognitive dysfunction.

A 'rational polypharmacy' of atypical antipsychotic combinations will probably develop over time and with well-designed studies. The combination of two different atypical antipsychotics has been observed to enhance efficacy in some patients with suboptimal response to any single antipsychotic. For example, small doses of risperidone are often added to clozapine in clinical settings to enhance clozapine's effects on refractory schizophrenia because the strong dopamine antagonism by risperidone is advantageous in certain patients with severe positive symptoms. Combining the cognitive-enhancing profiles of two atypicals (for example, olanzapine and risperidone) can improve cognitive deficits that are not addressed by either drug alone. Combining two low doses of atypical antipsychotics may lessen or avoid the emergence of side effects of a high dose of a single antipsychotic. For example, in a patient who responded well to 140 mg/d of ziprasidone but had difficulty with insomnia, adding 200 mg of quetiapine at bedtime and decreasing the ziprasidone dose to 100 mg solved the insomnia problem while maintaining the patient's good clinical response.

There is one published (but not double-blind) trial of combining clozapine with quetiapine in patients who developed excessive weight gain and/or diabetes with clozapine. When the daily dose of clozapine was reduced from 600 mg to 300 or 400 mg and 300 to 400 mg of quetiapine was added, patients lost weight and the diabetes improved without a change in clinical response.

An example of 'irrational polypharmacy' is adding a drug to combat a serious side effect of an atypical antipsychotic. One such example: Adding topiramate (Topamax®; approved for epilepsy and known to cause weight loss as a side effect) for patients who become severely obese on olanzapine has several risks: (1) topiramate has some potentially serious side effects of its own, such as cognitive slowing; (2) topiramate adds to the cost management of the psychosis; and (3) topiramate is not approved for weight loss, and there is a medicolegal liability risk for the physician in case of any adverse effects to the patient. The clinically sound management decision in such patients is to switch them from olanzapine to an atypical antipsychotic that causes little or no weight gain. Just as patients are sometimes switched for lack of efficacy, they should be switched for safety and adverse health effects.

Switching Safely

The most practical time to switch a patient from one antipsychotic to another is on an inpatient unit, where the switch and titration can be done quickly under constant monitoring. However, many switches have to be done in an outpatient setting to combat inadequate efficacy or lack of tolerability. To protect the patient from relapse (the most important risk during the transition), the new antipsychotic should be added and titrated up to a therapeutic dose within 4 to 6 days; then, the previous antipsychotic can be tapered down gradually over 4 to 6 days. Patients are protected from relapse with this add-and-taper method because they always receive a full daily dose of an antipsychotic and will not experience withdrawal complications.

Pharmacoeconomics

Schizophrenia's direct and indirect costs to society are estimated to be about $40 billion to $70 billion a year, adjusting for inflation, in the United States. The cost of treating, housing, and caring for a person with schizophrenia before the advent of atypical antipsychotics was estimated at $35,000 a year. The largest expense during the lifetime of a patient with schizophrenia has always been inpatient hospitalization. Antipsychotic medications are a vital component of the successful management of schizophrenia, yet they account for only a small fraction of the total cost of the illness. The atypical antipsychotics were initially regarded as very expensive ($2,000 to $3,000 per year) compared to the older oral antipsychotics (about $100 a year), although not when compared to injectable depot haloperidol decanoate (about $1,500 a year). However, their broader efficacy, better safety, and improved tolerability and compliance have reduced rehospitalization by about 12 hospital days per patient per year, according to epidemiological studies. Thus, the atypical antipsychotics save about $12,000 a year in bed-days of care, four times the older antipsychotics' annual costs. Many 'mirror image' studies of the costs for patients with schizophrenia before and after the introduction of clozapine for the treatment of refractory schizophrenia revealed significant savings in the disease management costs of schizophrenia, although clozapine is quite expensive (about $6,000 to $9,000 a year).

Cost-effectiveness is only one component of the overall effectiveness of the atypical antipsychotics, which also includes alleviation of suffering and anguish for patients and their families, a reduced suicide rate, improvement of social and vocational functioning, and enhanced reintegration into the mainstream. Although the complete restoration of wellness in all patients remains to be achieved, significant strides have been made in enhancing the quality of life of many patients with schizophrenia.

The Future of Antipsychotic Therapy for Schizophrenia

Intense basic and clinical neuropharmacological research is being conducted to develop better treatments and perhaps even a cure for serious brain disorders such as schizophrenia. New mechanisms of action are being explored that radically transcend those of existing agents. The next generation of antipsychotics may be 'neurostabilizers' rather than receptor antagonists. They may target neurotransmitter pathways other than dopamine or serotonin, such as those of glutamate and NMDA. There is growing evidence that the currently used atypical antipsychotics may exert 'neuroprotective' effects by inducing neurogenesis in certain brain regions such as the hippocampus olfactory tubercle and periventricular area. Future antipsychotics may act as 'neurotropic' agents that may be administered even before the onset of psychosis (such as in the prodromal phase in adolescence) or earlier (postnatally and even in utero) for specifically identified at-risk individuals. Ultimately, the ideal antipsychotic will probably be designed to induce specific gene expression(s) early in development to prevent the massive neurodevelopmental pathology observed in schizophrenia. Until then, the clinical management of schizophrenia will include an optimal mix of pharmacotherapy and psychosocial treatment and rehabilitation.

Suggested Readings

Efficacy

Arvanitis LA, Miller B: Multiple fixed doses of "Seroquel" (quetiapine) in patients with acute exacerbation of schizophrenia: a comparison with haloperidol and placebo. The Seroquel Trial 13 Study Group. *Biol Psychiatry* 1997;42:233-246.

Brook S, Lucey JV, Gunn KP: Intramuscular ziprasidone compared with intramuscular haloperidol in the treatment of acute psychosis. *J Clin Psychiatry* 2000;61:933-941.

Conley RR, Kelly DL: Management of treatment resistance in schizophrenia. *Biol Psychiatry* 2001;50:898-911.

Conley RR, Mahmoud R: A randomized double-blind study of risperidone and olanzapine in the treatment of schizophrenia or schizoaffective disorder. *Am J Psychiatry* 2001;158:765-774.

Csernansky JG, Mahmoud R, Brenner R: A comparison of risperidone and haloperidol for the prevention of relapse in patients with schizophrenia. *N Engl J Med* 2002;346:16-22.

Daniel DG, Zimbroff DL, Potkin SG, et al: Ziprasidone 80 mg/day and 160 mg/day in the acute exacerbation of schizophrenia and schizoaffective disorder: a 6-week placebo-controlled trial. Ziprasidone Study Group. *Neuropsychopharmacology* 1999;20:491-505.

Geddes J, Freemantle N, Harrison P, et al: Atypical antipsychotics in the treatment of schizophrenia: systematic overview and meta-regression analysis. *BMJ* 2000;321:1371-1376.

Jain KK: An assessment of iloperidone for the treatment of schizophrenia. *Expert Opin Investig Drugs* 2000;9:2935-2943.

Kane J, Honigfeld G, Singer J, et al: Clozapine for the treatment-resistant schizophrenic. A double-blind comparison with chlorpromazine. *Arch Gen Psychiatry* 1988;45:789-796.

Kane JM: Pharmacologic treatment of schizophrenia. *Biol Psychiatry* 1999;46:1396-1408.

Kapur S, Seeman P: Does fast dissociation from the dopamine d(2) receptor explain the action of atypical antipsychotics? A new hypothesis. *Am J Psychiatry* 2001;158:360-369.

Kay SR, Fiszbein A, Opler LA: The positive and negative syndrome scale (PANSS) for schizophrenia. *Schizophr Bull* 1987; 13:261-276.

Lewis DA: Atypical antipsychotic medications and the treatment of schizophrenia [editorial]. *Am J Psychiatry* 2002;159:177-179.

Marder SR, Meibach RC: Risperidone in the treatment of schizophrenia. *Am J Psychiatry* 1994;151:825-835.

Stahl SM: Dopamine system stabilizers, aripiprazole, and the next generation of antipsychotics: part 2: illustrating their mechanism of action. *J Clin Psychiatry* 2001;62:923-924.

Tollefson GD, Beasley CM Jr, Tamura RN, et al: Olanzapine versus haloperidol in the treatment of schizophrenia and schizoaffective and schizophreniform disorders: results of an international collaborative trial. *Am J Psychiatry* 1997;154:457-465.

Tran PV, Hamilton SH, Kuntz AJ, et al: Double-blind comparison of olanzapine versus risperidone in the treatment of schizophrenia and other psychotic disorders. *J Clin Psychopharmacol* 1997; 17:407-418.

Wright P, Birkett M, David SR, et al: Double-blind, placebo-controlled comparison of intramuscular olanzapine and intramuscular haloperidol in the treatment of acute agitation in schizophrenia. *Am J Psychiatry* 2001;158:1149-1151.

Side Effects

Allison DB, Mentore JL, Heo M, et al: Antipsychotic-induced weight gain: a comprehensive research synthesis. *Am J Psychiatry* 1999;156:1686-1696.

Comptom MT, Miller AH: Sexual side effects associated with conventional and atypical antipsychotics. *Psychopharmacology Bull* 2001;35:89-108.

Coodin S: Body mass index in persons with schizophrenia. *Can J Psychiatry* 2001;46:549-555.

Glassman AH, Bigger JT Jr: Antipsychotic drugs: prolonged QTc interval, torsades de pointes, and sudden death. *Am J Psychiatry* 2001;158:1774-1782.

Kapur S, Seeman P: Does fast association from dopamine d(2) receptor explain the action of atypical antipsychotics? A new hypothesis. *Am J Psychiatry* 2001;158:360-369.

Kopala L, Good K, Fredrikson D, et al: Risperidone in first-episode schizophrenia: Improvement in symptoms and pre-existing extrapyramidal signs. *Int J Psychiatry Clin Pract* 1998;2(suppl):S19-S25.

Lindenmayer JP, Nathan AM, Smith RC: Hyperglycemia associated with the use of atypical antipsychotics. *J Clin Psychiatry* 2001;62(suppl 23):30-38.

Masana PS, Gupta S: Long-term adverse effects of novel antipsychotics. *J Psychiatr Pract* 2000;6:299-309.

McIntyre RS, McCann SM, Kennedy SH: Antipsychotic metabolic effects: weight gain, diabetes mellitus and lipid abnormalities. *Can J Psychiatry* 2001;46:273-281.

Melkersson KI, Hulting AL, Brismar KE: Elevated levels of insulin, leptin and blood lipids in olanzapine-treated patients with schizophrenia or related psychoses. *J Clin Psychiatry* 2000; 61:742-749.

Meltzer HY, Matsubara S, Lee JC: Classification of typical and atypical antipsychotic drugs on the basis of dopamine D-1, D-2, and serotonin2 pKi values. *J Pharmacol Exp Ther* 1989;251:238-246.

Muench J, Carey M: Diabetes mellitus associated with atypical antipsychotic medications: new case reports and review of the literature. *J Am Board Fam Pract* 2001;14:278-282.

Nasrallah HA, Mulvihill T: Iatrogenic disorders associated with conventional vs atypical antipsychotics. *Ann Clin Psychiatry* 2001;13:215-227.

Nasrallah HA, Perry CL, Love E, et al: Ethnicity differences in hypertriglyceridemia secondary to olanzapine treatment. *Schizophr Res* 2002;53:165-166.

Osser DN, Najarian DM, Dufresne RL: Olanzapine increases weight and serum triglyceride levels. *J Clin Psychiatry* 1999;60:767-770.

Stahl SM: Selecting an atypical antipsychotic by combining clinical experience with guidelines from clinical trials. *J Clin Psychiatry* 1999;60(suppl 10):31-41.

Taylor DM, McAskill R: Atypical antipsychotics and weight gain—a systematic review. *Acta Psychiatr Scand* 2000;101:416-432.

Wirshing DA, Wirshing WC, Kysar L, et al: Novel antipsychotics: comparison of weight gain liabilities. *J Clin Psychiatry* 1999; 60:358-363.

Chapter **9**

Psychosocial Treatments and Rehabilitation

S chizophrenia is a serious brain disorder whose primary treatment is pharmacologic. However, patients with schizophrenia also need comprehensive, lifelong management that addresses their biological, psychological, social, and vocational needs. The integration of pharmacotherapy with psychosocial treatment modalities is therefore essential to achieve the best possible outcomes.

Just as medications are indispensable but do not necessarily remit all the acute psychotic symptoms in every patient, psychosocial interventions are helpful but do not necessarily halt the patient's social and vocational decline after the onset of illness. The deterioration of functioning in patients with schizophrenia over the first few years of the illness is well known and may be very difficult to reverse even if the delusions and hallucinations are well controlled. Many researchers believe that cognitive dysfunction may be the key reason for the difficulties that patients with schizophrenia have in restoring their premorbid personal, social, and vocational levels of functioning or in going back to the school or college where they were enrolled at the time of their first psychotic break.

As discussed in Chapter 8, the older antipsychotics had minimal therapeutic impact on cognitive dysfunction in schizophrenia and therefore did not enable patients to learn, remember, and apply the insights and skills imparted by psychotherapy or rehabilitation. Without healthy cognition (attention, verbal memory, visuospatial skills, motor dexterity, and executive functions), it is difficult to lead a productive and independent life. The new generation of atypical antipsychotics, which have been shown in several studies to improve cognition, promises to increase the likelihood that patients with schizophrenia can retain and assimilate the content of psychosocial therapies and translate it into useful coping skills and daily habits in their lives.

Types of Psychosocial Treatments

Most of the psychosocial treatments used in schizophrenia are also used in other psychiatric disorders (Table 9-1). Historically, psychotherapy preceded the discovery of medications for the treatment of psychiatric disorders. However, not all therapies are suitable for schizophrenia, and some, like insight-oriented psychodynamic psychotherapy, have been shown to be ineffective. Only a few psychosocial approaches (eg, intensive case management) have been developed specifically for chronic and serious psychiatric disorders such as schizophrenia. The primary goal of psychosocial interventions in schizophrenia is to provide social support and an understanding of the illness and its management by emphasizing the importance of adherence to treatment, establishing rapport and a therapeutic alliance with the patient, encouraging social functions, helping the patient cope with the usual stresses of life as well as the special stresses of having a serious neuropsychiatric illness like schizophrenia, and fostering independence and mastery of the activities of daily living.

The most important feature for the successful design of these interventions is flexibility, to meet the specific needs and goals of the patient. The scope of psychosocial and rehabilitative interventions includes helping the patient function individually as well as within a family or small social circle and, ultimately, in larger social and vocational situations.

Table 9-1: Various Types of Psychosocial Treatments Used in Schizophrenia

Individual Psychotherapy
- Supportive
- Psychodynamic
- Cognitive-behavioral
- Personal
- Psychoeducational

Family Therapy
- Supportive
- Psychodynamic
- Psychoeducational
- Behavioral

Group Therapy
- Supportive
- Psychodynamic
- Psychoeducational
- Behavioral
- Multifamily

Social Skills Training
- Basic social skills
- Social problem-solving
- Cognitive remediation

Vocational Therapy
- Supported employment

Case Management
- Assertive community treatment (ACT)
- Routine case management

While the main goal may be the patient's reintegration into society, the package of interventions is designed around the smaller goals that the patient needs to achieve in order to reach that ultimate goal. At first, these goals will probably focus on functioning individually and include resolving symptoms; recovering from acute episodes; improving insight, mood, and social functioning; and preventing relapse. As the patient's functioning ability expands, interacting with a difficult relative in the house, singing in a chorus, going on a date, or applying for a job may eventually become achievable goals.

The package of interventions, along with specific components of each intervention, is tailored to the individual patient during the course of his or her illness. Needs and goals change, not only from patient to patient, but also within the same patient at different points in time. With these changes, the need for interventions also must be reassessed and treatment plans redesigned.

Therapeutic Strategies for Psychosocial Interventions and Rehabilitation

Cognitive-Behavioral Therapy

The principal goal of cognitive-behavioral therapy is to reduce the distress and interference with functioning caused by psychotic symptoms. The therapy also aims to reduce emotional disturbance and help the patient understand psychosis, thereby promoting the patient's active participation in his or her care and reducing the risk of relapse and level of social disability.

Even with the use of newer medications, 25% to 50% of people with chronic schizophrenia still experience residual symptoms that cause some distress and interfere with functioning. Additionally, there are some patients who will not take their medication consistently or correctly. Cognitive-behavioral therapy can help these patients develop methods to cope with breakthrough psychotic symptoms such as hallucinations and delusions.

Cognitive-behavioral therapists employ the patient's own thoughts, beliefs, and images as the core materials to identify thinking biases. When applied to the treatment of patients with schizophrenia, and hence to the stress-vulnerability model, cognitive-behavior therapy operates on the key principle that different factors exert their influence in different cases and at different times. The therapist aims to develop an individual account of a person's vulnerabilities, stresses, and responses and to help that person modify cognition and behavior accordingly.

In summarizing this approach, Garety et al stated, "The central assumption of cognitive-behavioral therapy is that people with psychosis, like all of us, are attempting to make sense of the world and their experiences. The meanings attributed to their experiences and the way they process them, together with their earlier personality development, will influence the expression and development of symptoms, emotional responses, and behavior. Helping people to become aware of the processes which influence their thoughts and emotions and to re-evaluate their views of themselves and the psychosis is therefore central to therapy. Cognitive-behavioral therapy combines approaches based on these cognitive models with interventions grounded in the stress vulnerability model."

The stages of cognitive-behavioral therapy in schizophrenia include: (1) engagement and assessment, with special attention to establishing empathy and working from the patient's own perspective to ensure tolerability of sessions and to develop shared goals; (2) development of cognitive-behavioral coping strategies, with the goal of manipulating factors that contribute to the appearance of symptoms; (3) development of an understanding of psychosis that the patient can internalize and accept without guilt or denial; (4) targeting of delusions and hallucinations, once a relationship with the patient is established and it is determined how far the patient's interpretation can be challenged; (5) targeting of negative self-evaluations, anxiety, and depression, which are common in schizophrenia; and (6) management of the risk of relapse and social disability. These stages of cognitive-behavioral therapy are not conducted in a truly linear manner, and stages or elements of them are often revisited or repeated, depending on the patient's needs and goals.

Cognitive-behavioral therapy has been effective in treating negative and positive medication-resistant symptoms of schizophrenia. Cognitive-behavioral therapy can reduce or eliminate delusions and hallucinations, but it may be more effective against delusions. Reductions have also been seen in depression scores and in overall relapse rates in patients who undergo cognitive-behavioral therapy. However, no related improvement in social functioning has been seen, and no significant benefit over supportive therapy has been observed.

Individual Psychotherapy

Studies have shown that intensive, psychodynamically oriented psychotherapy is not appropriate for most patients with schizophrenia. Supportive therapy is therefore preferred. Goals of supportive therapy are to help the patient manage life stressors, to improve the patient's social and vocational functioning, and to help the patient develop a sense of control and increased self-esteem.

Individual supportive therapy requires the therapist to have a comprehensive understanding of the patient and his or her individual needs. This includes knowledge of the patient's internal psychiatric conflicts and defenses, the patient's coping skills and strengths, and the interpersonal, cultural, and biological factors that affect the patient's life. The therapist is important in establishing continuity of care for the patient and often assumes a coach-like or parent-like relationship.

Group Psychotherapy

For many patients, group therapy can be at least as effective as individual treatment. Some of the advantages for patients in group therapy include lower cost, social interaction, and peer support. Group therapy provides a supportive social network and is an especially good venue for teaching coping and interpersonal skills.

Some patients are more likely to benefit from group interactions. For example, group interactions can help reduce feelings of isolation, shame, guilt, and embarrassment in patients recovering from their first psychotic episode. Patients may be more amenable to observations and criticisms from peers rather than a therapist.

Group therapy can range from highly structured behavior therapy groups to less structured social groups, depending on the patients' needs. Goals tend to be less insight oriented and to focus on problem solving, goal planning, social interactions, and medication and side-effect management. If group therapy is the primary therapy, individual sessions can be incorporated based on each patient's needs.

Family Therapy

Historically, the family was blamed when schizophrenia afflicted one of its members. This faulty and devastating model has evolved into a model in which the family is involved in the long-term management of schizophrenia in a son or daughter and provided with support, education, and hope. The concept of 'expressed emotions' (EE) in some families of people with schizophrenia developed over the last 3 decades (Leff 1996) as a predictor of relapse even in adequately medicated patients, but it was later found to occur in many other psychiatric and nonpsychiatric illnesses. Therefore, the field has moved to family therapy as one of the important psychosocial interventions in schizophrenia. The emergence of strong family-driven advocacy groups such as the National Alliance for the Mentally Ill (NAMI) has been instrumental in peer education and support for families of the mentally ill and in advocacy for improved care for schizophrenia and other neurobiological mental disorders.

The focus of family therapy is to educate and foster hopeful and realistic expectations for the future. Additionally, the therapist determines family members' expectations of their role in the patient's care and develops coping strategies to help families manage problem behaviors. The therapist addresses family issues in terms of interaction with the patient. The therapist is there to understand and empathize with the family and to provide resources for support services and advocacy opportunities as a possible outlet.

When family interventions are added to maintenance medications, intervals between relapses become longer, giving patients time to reestablish social relations and to improve existing skills and develop new ones. Another advantage is continuity of care over long periods from the therapist. Family therapy also provides the opportunity for the therapist to enroll family members as part of the patient's treatment team. The family can be especially useful for encouraging compliance and can recognize early (prodromal) symptoms or relapse.

Essential components of successful family therapy include: (1) educating about schizophrenia, (2) teaching problem solving, (3) improving communications, (4) dealing with emotional issues, (5) encouraging family members to establish extended social networks, (6) lowering expectations to sustain the family's optimism over long periods of time, and (7) serving as the family's central contact to navigate bureaucracy and mobilize available and needed services.

Social Skills Training

Social skills training is a structured educational procedure that stresses the use of modeling, role playing, and social reinforcement. It is also referred to as *assertiveness training, personal effectiveness training,* and *structured learning therapy.* Social interactions, such as making a date or cashing a check, are broken down into smaller essential elements, such as maintaining eye contact and providing social reinforcement. Patients are taught first to perform the elements and then gradually to combine them to complete an entire interaction.

Social skills training resembles a classroom experience rather than a therapy session. Several models use role playing, modeling, reinforcement, and, often, videotaping to offer patients feedback and instruction. All methods can vary in length, depending on the patient's level of concentration and attention. The training also includes assessment, in which methods ranging from self-report inventories to direct observation are used.

The 'basic social skills training model' teaches specific verbal and nonverbal social skills, such as smiling, using the appropriate voice volume and speech duration, asking questions, and giving compliments. Role-playing sessions are usually followed by corrective feedback framed with praise, and corrective actions are often suggested as homework assignments. The 'social problem-solving model' includes many of the basic model's principles but focuses on helping patients manage unrehearsed social situations. This model divides the skills necessary for effective interpersonal communication: receiving, processing, and sending. A series of training modules addresses a variety of social and living skills specific to patients with schizophrenia, such as medication management, money management, grooming and self-care, and social problem-solving, and includes a patient workbook, an instructor's guide, and videotaped skills demonstrations. The modules are designed for use in small groups during 1-hour sessions.

The 'attention-focusing model' was developed for chronic psychiatric patients with severe cognitive, memory, and attention impairments that prevent them from being able to participate in standard social skills approaches that require active group participation. This model is characterized by the use of many short training trials and is generally used to teach conversational skills. It often uses food or drink in place of social reinforcement.

Social skills training favorably affects behavioral measures of social skills, self-ratings of assertiveness, and hospital discharge rates. When combined with day treatment, social skills training has been associated with moderately better social adjustment and competence achieved in a shorter amount of time. Most studies demonstrate no differences in relapse rates with social skills training; however, most of these studies involved brief, time-limited courses of treatment. Some investigators emphasize that a brief psychosocial intervention is no more likely to be effective at offering sustained improvement of schizophrenia than is a brief course of pharmacotherapy.

Vocational Rehabilitation

The ability to hold some type of active employment can increase a patient's commitment to treatment interventions and compliance. Additionally, the ability to contribute to the household and community through work enhances patient self-esteem and promotes reintegration into the community. In some cases, the added income may help ease financial burdens. However, positive and negative symptoms of schizophrenia often prevent employment in a competitive work force. Vocational rehabilitation for patients with schizophrenia is progressive; the patient is reintroduced first to work skills and eventually to full-time employment. Models of vocational rehabilitation vary in the degree to which they rely on community placement to achieve vocational outcomes.

As the length of inpatient stays has decreased, interest in hospital-based programs has waned. Many believe these programs may encourage institutional dependency in patients with schizophrenia. Sheltered workshops, which provide shortened work days, decreased on-the-job pressures, simplified tasks, and a structured, positive work environment, can be a good first step for many patients with schizophrenia who are not ready for competitive employment. But many believe that to be as effective as transitional skill-training environments, sheltered workshops must be embedded in a community support system with a full spectrum of rehabilitative services. Many variations on the living-working-socializing model exist. However, although these programs report higher employment rates among those who use them, no controlled data are available to offer information about other measures of outcome.

Psychosocial rehabilitation centers are informal, clubhouse settings in which participants are 'members.' The centers provide social and vocational services to residents in the form of on-site prevocational work to transitional employment. These programs have not demonstrated effectiveness in increasing members' ability to obtain competitive employment, but they have helped reduce hospitalization rates. In transitional employment programs, members spend half-days at the clubhouse and half-days in part-time jobs within the community. This 'bridge to competitive employment' offers support for members on the job and opportunities for community-based vocational assessment. The method seems to be effective in enabling members to secure employment and to hold employment for short periods of time.

Assertive community treatment (ACT), a case management approach that takes mobile treatment teams into the community to provide ongoing treatment services, often incorporates a vocational intervention. These interventions can include assisting patients with job-seeking and maintenance skills and may involve competitive, volunteer, or sheltered work experiences. Stein and Test's (P)ACT program emphasizes community-based vocational assessments, employs vocational counselors, and has a large network of job-placement sites. The effectiveness of other ACT programs for achieving vocational outcomes is less certain because many programs do not emphasize vocational goals, and many that do depend on community resources to provide job placement.

Supported employment programs provide ongoing job support for long-term employment for patients with severe mental illness. These programs may range from instruction about hygiene and social skills to providing transportation and on-site job support. Most research and funding sources have been in application for the mentally retarded population. However, limited studies in the late 1990s indicate that this rapid placement with ongoing support offers the best opportunity for patients with chronic mental illness such as schizophrenia, bipolar disorder, and related psychoses to maintain a regular job in the community. Particularly, supported employment programs that use the place-and-train vocational model can help patients obtain competitive entry-level employment. There is no evidence, however, that these programs lead to longer-term benefits for patients who may be able to progress beyond these positions.

Case Management

Case management originated shortly after care of the mentally ill shifted from institution-based to community-based patient rehabilitation. As psychiatric care services and resources became more fragmented, many patients needed an advocate to coordinate care. Clinical case management, which includes all aspects of the patient's physical and social environment—including housing, psychiatric treatment, general health care, welfare entitlements, transportation, and family and social networks—has become one of the preferred models for management of adults with severe mental illness.

There are several variations on the clinical management model. The psychosocial rehabilitation model combines rehabilitation assessment and planning, coordinating and linking patients with community services, and monitoring progress and advocacy. The strengths model focuses on the patient's strengths and self-determination, the case manager-patient relationship, and aggressive outreach. The most popular model is ACT. This model includes assertive outreach, teaching and assistance in daily living skills, 24-hour coverage 7 days a week, assistance in finding work, and a focus on the patient's strengths. ACT assigns each patient to a multidisciplinary team that has a fixed case load and a high staff-to-patient ratio and that delivers all services when and where the patient needs them.

The possibilities afforded to the patient with schizophrenia make case management a valuable resource. However, schizophrenia poses its own unique challenges to case management models. Patients with schizophrenia require a higher level of attention than the traditional single case-manager approach can offer. ACT programs seem to hold the most promise for offering the level of care a patient with schizophrenia requires for successful reintegration.

There are several features of case management that increase its likelihood of success. Small caseload is essential; one case manager for each 10 to 15 patients is considered the optimal ratio. When caseloads become larger, the case manager becomes reactive rather than proactive in patient care. Case managers can best serve patients where resources are available and easily accessed. In areas where there are few or no resources for the patient to use, the benefit of having a case manager to link patients to services is limited.

With regard to efficacy and effectiveness, there is a significant reduction in hospitalization. The ACT model, compared with standard care, offers the most impressive evidence for reduced hospital admissions and duration of stay. Case management does not seem to significantly improve clinical or social outcome. However, ACT has shown advantages over standard care in its participants' housing situation and employment. Case management also seems to have no effect on quality-of-life parameters, although patients report more satisfaction in intensive case management than in standard care. While many studies do not report medication compliance in terms of case management, patients receiving ACT are more likely to have good adherence to treatment.

Conclusion

The success of second-generation antipsychotics in reducing or eliminating patients' positive symptoms, improving cognition, and reducing side effects allows the opportunity to evolve psychosocial treatments that were not possible before in the management of schizophrenia. As more second-generation antipsychotics are developed and more positive results are obtained, the future of research into combining pharmacotherapy with psychosocial treatment and rehabilitation seems promising.

Lasting integration of patients with schizophrenia requires a collaboration between psychiatric and rehabilitative staff to provide patients with the resources they need for success. Psychiatric medicine provides promising pharmacotherapeutic therapies as well as psychotherapeutic services that have proven effective in reengaging patients with schizophrenia with their environment. We look to integrate these psychosocial care services with rehabilitation treatments that offer social skills, vocational skills, and case-management services. Together, this 'rehabilitation alliance' can offer patients the skills crucial to function—to work, to love, to play—and to live life to its fullest.

Suggested Readings

Aquila R, Santos G, Malumud T, et al: The rehabilitation alliance in practice: the clubhouse connection. *Psychiatr Rehab J* 1999;60(suppl 19):23-29.

Aquila R, Weiden PJ, Emanuel M: Compliance and the rehabilitation alliance. *J Clin Psychiatry* 1999;60(suppl 19):23-29.

Bond GR, Dietzen LL, McGrew JH, et al: Accelerating entry into supported employment for persons with severe psychiatric disabilities. *Rehabil Psychol.* In press.

Bustillo JR, Lauriello J, Horan WP, et al: The psychosocial treatment of schizophrenia: An update. *Am J Psychiatry* 2001;158:163-175.

Garety PA, Fowler D, Kuipers E: Cognitive-behavioral therapy. In: Lieberman JA, Murray R, eds. *Comprehensive Care of Schizophrenia: A Textbook of Clinical Management.* London, Blackwell Science (US Distribution), 2001, p 97.

Leff J: First perceptions of treatment: the physician-family-patient network. *J Pract Psychiatry Behavioral Health* 1996;2:10-15.

Lieberman JA, Murray R, eds: *Comprehensive Care of Schizophrenia: A Textbook of Clinical Management.* London, Blackwell Science (US Distribution), 2001.

Sensky T, Turkington D, Kingdon D, et al: A randomized controlled trial of cognitive-behavioral therapy for persistent symptoms in schizophrenia resistant to medication. *Arch Gen Psych* 2000;57:165-172.

Shriqui CL, Nasrallah HA, eds: *Contemporary Issues in the Treatment of Schizophrenia.* Washington, DC, American Psychiatric Press, 1995.

Weiden PJ, Scheifler PL, Diamond RJ, et al: *Breakthroughs in Antipsychotic Medications: A Guide for Consumers, Families, and Clinicians.* New York, WW Norton, 1999.

Index

A

E

NOTES